LI

FROM

DARKNESS

✳

Nine Times the Catholic Church
Was in Turmoil—and Came Out
Stronger Than Before

✳

STEVE WEIDENKOPF

Catholic
Answers
Press

Published by Catholic Answers, Inc.
2020 Gillespie Way
El Cajon, California 92020
1-888-291-8000 orders
619-387-0042 fax
catholic.com

Printed in the United States of America
Cover by Claudine Mansour Design
Cover photograph by Cristina Gottardi/Unsplash
Interior by Russell Graphic Design

978-1-68357-249-7
978-1-68357-250-3 Kindle
978-1-68357-251-0 ePub

To Joe and Cathy Burns

For the beautiful example of your marriage rooted in Christ, nourished by the sacraments of the Church, and lived in fidelity, unity, and charity. For your friendship, support, and prayers through the years and for introducing us to Van and Davy.

May we always live Under the Mercy.

Although the world of today has a very vivid awareness of its unity and of how one man depends on another in needful solidarity, it is most grievously torn into opposing camps by conflicting forces. Influenced by such a variety of complexities, many of our contemporaries are kept from accurately identifying permanent values and adjusting them properly to fresh discoveries. As a result, buffeted between hope and anxiety and pressing one another with questions about the present course of events, they are burdened down with uneasiness. This same course of events leads men to look for answers; indeed, it forces them to do so.

—Gaudium et Spes 4

CONTENTS

ACKNOWLEDGMENTS

My ability to write, teach, and help Catholics learn the real story of Church history is not possible without the love, support, and prayers of my beautiful wife, Kasey. I am grateful for the patience and understanding exhibited by my children during the writing of this book. Thanks are also in order to Todd Aglialoro for accepting the proposal for this unique work. I also want to acknowledge the people I have met and talked with during my years of speaking at parishes and conferences who asked questions about the past and the present. Their curiosity and desire for my opinion on a host of topics helped me develop the idea for this book.

Lastly, I give thanks for St. Catherine of Siena, a spunky laywoman alive during a tumultuous time in Church history, who was not afraid to call for worldly and spiritual reform but who placed her hope entirely in the bosom of Jesus. Her intercession enabled the completion of this project.

INTRODUCTION

A decade into the fifth century, Alaric the Goth sacked the city of Rome. The event caused consternation throughout the world and people searched for explanations for how something previously unthinkable became reality. When news reached an irascible translator of Scripture in Bethlehem named Jerome, he wept bitterly. The scholar struggled to comprehend how an army of Visigoths, warriors who had recently fought for the Roman Empire, could sack the historic city. Although Jerome's reaction was understandable, the city's sacking should not have been a surprise. A review of imperial actions toward the Germanic tribes on the borders in the recent past would have equipped Jerome to predict the destruction of Rome. However, Jerome was focused on the present and could not anticipate it—or at least not fail to be surprised by it. But if he had been equipped with historical perspective and context, he could have been spared much of the anguish caused by the devastating news of Rome's ruin.

A historical perspective of Roman relations with the Germanic tribes on the frontier would have helped Jerome remember, for example, the annihilation of three Roman army legions at the Battle of Teutoburg Forest in A.D. 9. Arminius, a chief of the Germanic Cherusci tribe, who had been a hostage in the imperial capital as a boy, served the empire in the Roman army.[1] He was ordered to Germania to help the Romans subdue the populace but did not forget his origins; so instead, he secretly planned the defeat of the legions. Arminius's victory ended Roman plans for conquest east of the Rhine River, which became the natural border between the empire and the northern Germanic hordes. The Romans built forts and outposts along the Rhine, which later became major European cities, to control the Germans and guard the empire against invasion.

Over the centuries, Germanic tribes along the border grew restless and desired admittance into the empire in order to enjoy its economic, political, and military benefits. Many were allowed entrance in the later fourth and early fifth centuries, as Rome turned to these warriors to provide needed manpower to staff the army. Roman anxiety concerning the Germanic peoples remained, however, and the barbarian warriors were usually treated as auxiliary troops attached to imperial units rather than as regular army units. This arrangement worked for a time until Alaric, a Romanized commander of Gothic auxiliary troops, demanded greater recognition for his troops' courage and sacrifice. When Roman officials refused, Alaric unleashed his warriors on the majestic imperial city.

Alaric's sack produced different reactions throughout the empire. While Jerome wept in Bethlehem, others turned to anger. Despite the legalization of the Catholic Church nearly a century prior and its recognition as the official religion of the empire thirty years before, paganism still existed in the Roman world. As they had in the Church's early centuries, pagans again placed blame on Christians for the destruction of the imperial capital, claiming that nothing so catastrophic had happened to Rome when the empire worshipped the old gods. The false idea that the empire flourished only until it embraced the Christian faith gained favor in public discourse and demanded a response. St. Augustine (354–430) addressed these criticisms in his influential work *The City of God*.

The City of Man and the City of God

Augustine's *magnum opus* not only answered the immediate objections of his contemporaries; it provided (and provides) a foundation of authentic Christian historical perspective. As a young man, Augustine had known well the pagan mentality, as he rejected the Faith and embraced the cults of false gods. Eventually, through the patient prayers of his saintly mother Monica, Augustine converted and found peace. The pagan scapegoating of the Church disturbed Augustine, so he dedicated thirteen years to writing a response and developing a Catholic understanding of history. Subtitled *Against the Pagans*, the *City of God* is a Catholic manifesto on interpreting history and maintaining a proper perspective of human events.

The work comprises two parts containing twenty-two books. Part one (books I–X) articulates a defense of the Faith in response to the pagan charge that the Church was the reason for the empire's decay. Part two (XI–XXII), which forms the majority of the work, illustrates Augustine's historical perspective, wherein history is viewed as a great drama between two cities: the City of Man and the City of God. The City of Man, founded on self-love, is where pride, ambition, greed, and expediency reign supreme. In contrast, the City of God is founded on self-lessness and love of God, and in it humility, sacrifice, and obedience are paramount.

Membership in the City of God is not exclusionary. As Augustine wrote: "So long, then, as the heavenly City is wayfaring on earth, she invites citizens from all nations and all tongues, and unites them into a single pilgrim band."[2] The cities are distinct yet comingled in time. Each individual struggles with membership in both cities. At times, the citizen finds himself immersed in the City of Man and at other times he is safely ensconced in the City of God, but, more often than not, he bestrides the two. Augustine's construct is meant to illustrate that the "meaning of history lies not in the flux of outward events, but in the hidden drama of sin and redemption."[3] For Augustine, the sack of Rome, as devastating as it was, did not constitute the end of the world, as some feared, nor a repudiation of the Faith, as the pagans claimed. Rather, the event can be understood through the prism of an authentic historical perspective as the free-willed action of inhabitants of the City of Man, focused on selfish goals.

Embracing Augustine's perspective gives us the ability to maintain calm and hope in the midst of earthly calamities. Sadly, that perspective is sorely lacking in the modern age.

Modernity has lost a proper sense of historical perspective and lacks historical memory. Perhaps this mindset is widespread because modern man is too entrenched in the City of Man and has rejected, or at least ignores, the City of God. The Catholic author, historian, and politician Hilaire Belloc (1870–1953) opined on this modern mindset in his 1929 work *Survivals and New Arrivals*. In it he analyzed the strength and vitality of the Church in the modern world by focusing on the various forms of attacks against it and how likely the Church was to survive these assaults. He categorized these attacks into *survivals* and *new arrivals*. Survivals were centuries-old attacks that were not sustainable into the future. The main opposition came from the new arrivals: attacks present in Belloc's day, such as nefarious political ideologies that seek to replace the Church with the state as the citizen's object of love and obedience. Within this group Belloc included also the modern mind, which he qualified as not so much an attack as a *resistance*—something that tries to render faith unintelligible. With its three main vices of pride, ignorance, and intellectual sloth, the modern mind impedes a vibrant faith life.

It also views history with disdain, believing that modernity is superior to the past. As a result, the present becomes the sole focus of human activity and thought. Reflection on the past in order to learn from history is rejected. The future is ignored because it cannot produce immediate and tangible results. God is ignored, partly because the principal benefit of a relationship with him is in the future (eternal life), and instead, modern man worships himself. Belloc argued that changing the modern mind proves extremely difficult, because indoctrination in this false mindset is achieved through universal compulsory education, which is centered on the accumulation of information rather than on forming virtue. Additionally, Belloc noted that the modern mind lacks the skill of critical thinking, in part, because it focuses on the pursuit of temporal pleasures in the present and because the popular press enables this "sloth by providing sensational substitutes."[4]

The Tyranny of the Present

Belloc's analysis of modernity is still strikingly relevant a century after his writing. Modern society is consumed with the immediate and rejects the past by either ignoring it, at best, or crafting a new narrative that undermines the actions and memory of previously important historical actors. As an example, there is a modern fascination with labeling Christopher Columbus (along with other explorers and missionaries) a genocidal maniac who sailed the ocean blue to enrich himself, enslave the native peoples of the New World, and spread disease, destruction, and death. Pope Benedict XVI noted modernity's obsession with the present and the consequences such a false orientation produces:

> The contemporary consumer society tends instead to relegate human beings to the present, to make them lose their sense of the past, of history; but by so doing it also deprives them of the ability to understand themselves, to perceive problems and to build the future . . . the

INTRODUCTION

> Christian is someone who has a good memory, who loves
> history and seeks to know it.[5]

The *tyranny of the present*, wherein man's focus is solely
on the now, enslaves modern man in a construct of his own
creation and prevents learning from the past and shaping the
future. The present sublimates all thought and activity away
from self-reflection. The rejection of historical memory
produces a lack of historical context, which culminates in
a lack of perspective of human events. Therefore, modern
man is unable to properly comprehend contemporary hap-
penings with a frame of historical reference and is enslaved
in the tyranny of the present. Modern man lacks perspective
of actions taking place in the modern world. The lack of
perspective, rooted in loss of historical memory, is perpetu-
ated by the popular press and its twenty-four-hour news
cycle of repetitive propaganda. It is nourished too by social
media, which are perhaps the quintessential tools of the tyranny of the present.

The loss of the historical past results in the vices of quick
judgments, false attribution of motives, and a general hermeneutic of suspicion. These attributes contribute to a negative discourse in which every word or action is interpreted
in the most extreme manner, producing shrill sensational
commentary that seeks to compel the attention of citizens
enslaved by the tyranny of the present. Every utterance of
a main actor (politicians, the pope) in the modern world
is broadcast widely and interpreted in a way that suits the

narrative of the presenter of the information. The tyranny of the present impedes our ability to read and hear in full context and develop a thoughtful reflection on what they say and do. Instead, we settle for tweets, clickbait headlines, and thirty-second soundbites steeped in a hermeneutic of suspicion. And the widespread ability in modern society for everyone to publish or broadcast an opinion on any subject leads to a cacophony of voices that are not focused on authentic interpretation of events with historical perspective but rather seek attention from others in a clash of wills. Those who shout the loudest with the most sensational interpretation receive the most attention, which feeds the need for similar behavior in the future.

The fruit of the tyranny of the present is *anxiety,* as modern man has no anchor upon which to safely understand present activity in the context of historical memory and perspective. And so modern man is no different from the pagans of Augustine's day who blamed the Church for Alaric's sack of Rome. We, too, lack a view of history with God at the center—a view that sees human events as part of the drama of sin and redemption—because we have rejected the Christian worldview that girded Western Civilization for centuries, and so we are rudderless in a sea of unease.

This modern mentality affects Catholics as well. Lacking historical perspective, we react to trials in the Church, such as clerical scandals, with anger and anxiety. Some Catholics, angry at the Church and its leaders, react by leaving the

Church. Others remain in the Church but criticize every utterance and action of the pope or bishop they do not agree with. Still others become convinced that the present trials must be the vanguard of some long-awaited mass apostasy or apocalyptic sequence.

What is the antidote to this tyranny of the present? *Knowledge of Church history*, which gives us a long-term perspective on God's divine plan.

Learning from the past is predicated on knowing the past. Shaping the future is rooted in a correct interpretation and perspective on modern events. Thus, the anxiety produced by living in the tyranny of the present can be overcome with knowledge that previous generations of Catholics lived through similar situations and prevailed. Historical memory and perspective also enable us to recognize that previous crises in Church history produced *renewal and reform*. From the darkness of men, God's light has emerged. He does not allow the darkness, even when it comes from high offices in the Church, to triumph.

Learning lessons from Church history requires acknowledgment that the Church is holy but its members are fallen (yet redeemed) creatures. The individual actions of Catholics impact the Church as a whole both positively and negatively, but the negative actions—even of popes and bishops—never invalidate the mission and holiness of the Church. Ultimately, knowing Church history should lead to a greater devotion to the Holy Spirit, who has guided, guarded, and animated the Church since Pentecost. "When one remembers how the Catholic Church has been governed, and by whom," Belloc aptly put it, "one realizes that it must be divinely inspired to have survived at all."[6]

Developing a Proper Historical Perspective

I am often asked whether things in the Church are worse now than they were in the past. Perhaps that question is asked from true curiosity but, I believe, it is usually asked because the inquirer lacks the historical perspective that would provide context to modern ecclesial events. There is no argument that the current state of the Church is cause for anxiety among the Catholic faithful. News reports of national bishops' conferences and synods proposing radical changes in ecclesiastical discipline strike fear in the hearts of the orthodox. Pagan ceremonies and idols in Rome spread confusion and anger. Some conclude the state of today's Church must be worse than it has ever been, and they bemoan a lack of leadership from the bishops.

And yet, although many modern events in the Church are troubling, a review of Church history provides examples of far-worse crises that threatened the Bride of Christ. This is not an empty platitude. To put it plainly, Church history shows that evil does not prevail. God, in his infinite love and mercy, brings good out of evil situations that, in the moment, and viewed without the proper historical perspective, might have seemed irreformable. There are plentiful examples of darkness in the Church's past, but, each time, God leads his people into light. Christians are people of hope, and to live that virtue authentically, we need the perspective of our history.

God does not abandon the Church, and neither should we.

In this book I have chosen to highlight nine Church crises. Each chapter provides the historical context of the time period involved, a detailed description of the crisis, and the story of the reform and renewal that occurred following the crisis. Another chapter is devoted to illustrating the proper (and improper) response of Catholics living in a time of ecclesial crisis utilizing the life and times of St. Catherine of Siena and the Florentine Dominican Savonarola.

It is my hope and prayer that this book may prove a compass for Catholics in the modern world in order to find succor in the lessons of history, grow in devotion to the Holy Spirit, and trust in Christ's mandate that the gates of hell will not prevail against his Church.

1

The *Lapsi*

Who could be so callous, so stony-hearted, who so unmindful
of brotherly love, as to remain dry-eyed in the presence of so
many of his own kin, who are broken now, shadows of their
former selves, disheveled, in the trappings of grief?[7]

—St. Cyprian

THE DARKNESS:
Roman persecution resulted not only in the death of
Christians but also in an internal division concerning the
proper response to those who apostatized and sought a
return to the Church after the persecution. The divergent
views created disunity that threatened to tear apart the
new Church.

THE LIGHT:
Through the pastoral ministry of various popes and bishops, the Church preached a unified message of mercy to

those who abandoned the Faith during Roman persecution. Their witness, teaching, and preaching developed Catholic understanding of penance and the role of the sacrament of confession in the life of the Church.

Background

The Church was born into the world of the Roman Empire. It was not obvious that a city in the middle of the Italian peninsula would launch and sustain a worldwide empire. In fact, the early Romans harbored no dreams of world domination; but over the centuries, the people of the city of seven hills crafted an impressive imperial system comprising forty provinces that sixty million people called home. Built on the bravery and savagery of the Roman army and encompassing a class-oriented society with a large slave population, the Roman Empire was enjoying a time of relative peace when a strange man in a backwater province appeared on the scene. The followers of the holy man claimed he rose from the dead and was God incarnate.

At first, the Romans believed these followers of Jesus, who were soon known as *Christians*, to be Jewish, since the movement originated in Judea and was mostly composed of Jews. However, righteous Gentiles joined the movement in large numbers, especially through the missionary activity of Paul of Tarsus, even as many Jews rejected the radical teaching of the apostles of Christ. Romans were a religious people, and they tolerated the different gods of their subjected peoples as long as they did not interfere with Roman peace and progress. The Jews, for example, were allowed to practice their unique faith and were not forced to worship the pantheon of Roman deities because the Romans respected the antiquity and ethnicity of the Jewish religion. The Romans believed a religion that could trace ancient origins was more authentic than a fad such as the new Christian movement.[8] As the Christian faith separated itself from its Jewish origins, it provoked Roman curiosity and suspicion. The former led to converts but the latter led to persecution.

In the middle of the first century, a psychopath who would later poison his brother, murder his mother, and kick his pregnant wife to death, ascended the imperial throne in Rome. At the young age of seventeen, Nero became "lord of the world" and his fourteen-year reign was a notorious orgy of debauchery, destruction, and death. A decade into Nero's rule, in the summer of A.D. 64, a conflagration engulfed the city of Rome, destroying large sections of the imperial capital. People were angry because the fire's cause was not natural. Rumors circulated that the mad emperor had ordered the blaze to make room for his grand vision of a new city named after himself, "Neropolis." Afraid to lose his grip on power, Nero quickly found a scapegoat to turn the gaze of the incensed Romans. As the Roman historian Tacitus records, Nero blamed the fire on the small group of Christians in the city and initiated the first of several persecutions.[9]

The blame game backfired on Nero as many Romans saw through his weak attempt to deflect criticism. The manner of Christian resoluteness in the face of severe torture and sadistic executions moved the Romans to pity. Nevertheless, Nero's localized persecution of the Church in Rome had far-reaching impacts. The imperial violence took the lives of the two great apostles and Church leaders, Peter and Paul. Additionally, Nero outlawed the Christian faith, placing the Church squarely in the crosshairs of imperial authorities; a situation not rectified for nearly 300 years.

During the next several centuries, Roman authorities persecuted the Catholic Church in waves of sporadic harassment. Many persecutions were localized to a particular province and there were even times of relative peace for Christians. Indeed, after Nero's persecution the next significant act of governmental violence didn't occur for half a century: in Antioch with the arrest and eventual death of St. Ignatius of Antioch in the Flavian amphitheater. After that, a generation passed before another major Christian figure was killed: Polycarp, the aged bishop of Smyrna and disciple of St. John, was made a martyr in the mid-second century when a Roman mob celebrating a festival in honor of the emperor demanded Christian blood.

The early Church suffered not only external governmental persecution but also internal dissension. In the late second century a believer named Montanus claimed direct revelation from the Holy Spirit and advocated his personal revelation as equal in authority to Scripture and the teaching of the Church. Montanus and his followers lived a strict ascetical life, which gave the outward appearance of holiness, rooted in severe penitential discipline with an emphasis on fasting.

Among his more radical teachings, he urged his followers to seek out martyrdom from imperial officials—an exhortation the Church did not embrace. The example of Montanism illustrates how the early Church contained radical elements bent on pursuing their own agendas and manner of Christian living outside the confines of Church authority and teaching.

And then, as the Church moved into the third century of existence, bishops faced a momentous question concerning the reconciliation of Christians who gave in to Roman persecution and apostatized, radical opinions on the question divided the people of God and severely tested the hierarchy.

Crisis

At the end of the first century, Christians numbered less than 10,000 in the Roman Empire but the effects of missionary activity and the working of the Holy Spirit increased that number substantially in the second. The Church counted 200,000 members at the beginning of the third century and by midcentury a Christian population boom increased that number to more than a million, or nearly two percent of the imperial population.[10] With increased numbers came increased imperial attention and major internal questions to answer. The third century of Christian experience was one of turmoil, with controversies concerning the explanation of doctrine, disputes about Christian living, and debate over the role of the bishop of Rome.[11] This is the century of the first antipope and first schism in Church history, which both resulted from a fundamental question concerning sin and penance.

The early Church recognized the power given by Christ to the clergy to forgive sins and reconcile the sinner to God through the sacrament of penance, but questions surrounded penitential practices and whether sins committed after baptism could be forgiven. The early Christian apologist and theologian Tertullian (163–230), the son of a Roman army centurion, identified one early penitential practice known as the *exomologesis* in his work *De Penitentia*, written in the early third century. The *exomologesis* consisted of a public penitential act preceded by a declaration of sin to the bishop, who determined the penance required of the penitent. Upon its completion, the repentant sinner was welcomed back into communion by the bishop in a public setting. During the period of penance, the Christian wore simple clothes, was not allowed to receive the Eucharist, and begged fellow Christians attending Mass for their prayers.[12]

Usually the *exomologesis* was undertaken once, although it was possible to repeat it if necessary. Tertullian expressed concern with granting repeated access to the *exomologesis,* believing it could lead the faithful to sin more frequently if they knew there was an avenue of forgiveness. One significant caveat to the *exomologesis* was that it was not available for every sin, notably excluding apostasy, idolatry, murder, and fornication. However, Pope St. Callistus I (r. 217–222) allowed those who committed sexual sins to participate in the *exomologesis*, a decision rooted in mercy that angered many Christians, including Tertullian and the Roman priest Hippolytus.

Hippolytus was a "rigorist" who argued that the *exomologesis* should not be modified, even if the bishop of Rome decided to do so for good pastoral reasons. He was so angry at the papal decision that he gathered a group of followers who elected him pope, becoming the first—but unfortunately not the last—antipope. Hippolytus claimed that Callistus, a former slave, was unworthy of the papal office because in his former life he had been accused of embezzlement. Hippolytus's schism lasted for nineteen years and through the pontificates of Callistus, St. Urban I (r. 222–230), and St. Pontian (r. 230–235).

Years later, during the imperial reign of Maximinus Thrax, another wave of Christian persecution targeting the clergy erupted. The reigning pope, Pontian, and antipope Hippolytus were arrested and sent to the mines on the island of Sardinia. Amid the suffering and hardship of the mines, Hippolytus renounced his schism and papal claim and was reconciled to the Church. Pontian and Hippolytus both succumbed to the harsh conditions and their bodies were transported for burial in Rome, where they were recognized as martyrs and saints of the Church. St. Hippolytus, the first antipope, also became the only antipope in Catholic history to be canonized!

The questions concerning sin and penance took on greater urgency in the mid-third century after the persecution of Decius (r. 249–251). That emperor was a strong and inflexible man who desired unity in the empire. Confronted with serious political and military issues and even natural disaster, he sought unity in the empire and the pacification of the pagan gods. So, in January 250 he issued an edict that required every citizen in the empire to make a public sacrifice to them. Decius's persecution did not target Christians specifically, as sacrifice was required by all, but he definitively wanted Christians to conform to the common imperial cults. The emperor sought Christian apostates, not martyrs; his persecution resulted in both and produced a massive crisis that threatened to shred Christian unity.

All those who sacrificed received a certificate, known as the *libellus*, documenting their adherence to Decius's edict. Commissions were established in cities and towns to record the sacrifices and issue the certificates. Failure to comply with the imperial edict involved confiscation of property along with the possibility of imprisonment, torture, and even execution. In the persecution's earliest stages, the church in Rome was greatly impacted by the death of Pope St. Fabian (r. 236–250), who refused to sacrifice and was martyred. Other Christians, however, including bishops, offered the sacrifice in order to save their lives. There was even a report of one bishop who walked up to the imperial authorities with a lamb under his arm for the sacrifice![13] Wealthy Christians offered bribes to others to sacrifice in their name or had their slaves sacrifice, believing that it spared them moral culpability. They received the *libellus*, and were known as *libellatici*, but they had not actually sacrificed. These *libellatici* were criticized for their cowardice, as evidenced in a letter from a bishop in Carthage: "Many were defeated before the battle was joined, they collapsed without any encounter, thus even depriving themselves of the plea that they had sacrificed to the idols against their will. Without any compulsion they hastened to the forum."[14] Many Christians resisted, but many apostatized and sacrificed; these were known as the *sacrificati*.

Others fled the cities in order to avoid confrontation with imperial authorities. Thascius Caecilianus Cyprianus (Cyprian), bishop of Carthage, was one. He fled to the desert knowing that his position as bishop would draw the attention of the empire. Cyprian believed he could more effectively exhort and support his flock during the persecution through public letters. It was out of prudence rather than cowardice, therefore, that Cyprian sought exile during the persecution, as he explained in a later letter: "The crown is bestowed at God's good pleasure and is not received till the appointed hour, so that if a man, abiding in Christ withdraws for a while, he is not denying his faith but only awaiting the time."[15]

Cyprian's refuge in the desert during the persecution proved providential, as his letters give us great insight into the daily life of a third-century particular church in the midst of imperial harassment. Cyprian was well educated and before his conversion had a career as a gifted orator and teacher of rhetoric. The self-assured rhetorician, who had converted to the Christian faith in 246 through the influence of the priest Caecilianus, became disillusioned and angry at the rampant corruption, savagery, bribery, and sexual promiscuity of Roman society. He gave his wealth to the poor, and soon after his conversion was ordained a priest and just a few years later he was elected bishop of Carthage. Cyprian was an avid reader and admirer of the works of Tertullian, but unlike his fellow Carthaginian, Cyprian did not embrace a rigorist position toward those who apostatized during the persecution.

The presence of large numbers of Christians who "lapsed" (the *lapsi*) resulted in an "unprecedented crop of more or less nominal apostasies, and the anomalous situation arose that in many places the majority of the faithful, guilty of a sin the Church refused to pardon, were out of the Church."[16] Because apostates were not admitted to the *exomologesis*, despite their contrition, the practice developed whereby the *lapsi* asked Christians suffering for the Faith (through imprisonment and/or execution) during persecution—known as the *confessors*—to pray for them and request their readmittance to communion. However, problems arose when the confessors began to view this privilege as a right and ordered bishops to reinstate sinners. Additionally, the confessors' intercession on behalf of an individual penitent soon morphed into blanket letters to be used by anyone, thus usurping the authority of the bishops to oversee the penitential process.

In order to stop the unauthorized action of the confessors, Cyprian excommunicated those in Carthage who continued the practice. Recognizing the significant pastoral problems brought about by the persecution, Cyprian urged patience and mercy for the *lapsi*. He modified the stringent rule forbidding apostates from readmittance to communion by allowing *lapsi* in grave illness or near death to return to the Church, a practice he imported from the Roman church. Cyprian made this concession with the understanding that once the persecution ended and he and other bishops in the region could return safely to their sees, they would gather to discuss the *lapsi* and develop a unified policy.

The persecution of Decius finally abated when the tyrant, along with his son, was killed by the Goths on campaign in the Balkans—the first Roman emperor to die by the hands of a foreign enemy. The end of the persecution allowed Cyprian to return to Carthage, where he held a synod of regional bishops (sixty in total) to develop a pastoral plan to handle the *lapsi*. The assembled bishops agreed to decide cases of the *lapsi* on an individual basis while also confirming the previous policy of allowing *lapsi* in danger of death immediate readmittance. The bishops also decided that *sacrificati* (those who had actually sacrificed to the pagan gods) had to perform penance for their sins for the remainder of the lives and only be allowed readmittance before death. Additionally, the bishops ruled that *lapsi* must perform penance in order to return to the Church; pardon from a confessor was not sufficient.

Some *libellatici* complained bitterly that they were lumped in with the *sacrificati* in being required to perform penance. Cyprian addressed this complaint in a direct manner in a letter: "Nor let people flatter themselves that they need do no penance because they have kept their hands clean from the accursed sacrifices, when all the time they have certificates of sacrifice on their conscience. Why, such a certificate is itself a confession of apostasy."[17] He remarked also that obtaining a certificate without the stain of sacrificing was still sinful, even if the guilt was lessened, and urged the *libellatici* to "persevere in doing penance and imploring God's mercy."[18] The decisions at the synod were compiled and sent to the Roman church for its awareness. But although Cyprian and the bishops in other areas of the Church believed that a pastoral policy for the *lapsi* would bring unity and peace to the faithful, there were those who chose the path of disagreement and confrontation.

Opposing groups quickly developed in the Church concerning the *lapsi,* and their unwavering opinions proved problematic for the pope and other bishops. One group argued against any accommodation for the *lapsi*, even if they were repentant. This rigorist position argued against clemency believing that the sin of apostasy could not be forgiven. These rigorists believed that the Church could only intercede for God's mercy on the *lapsi.* Rigorism gained adherents because many Christians maintained the Faith and suffered during the persecution, perhaps even losing family members to martyrdom, and it seemed unjust to allow readmittance to those who had lapsed now that the threat of suffering was passed. When Pope St. Fabian (r. 236–250) died, rigorists hoped for one of their own to replace him, but instead St. Cornelius (r. 251–253) was chosen, and they became enraged when Cornelius embraced the way of mercy and allowed apostates to participate in the *exomologesis.*

In response, they decided to "elect" the priest and distinguished theologian Novatian as pope. Following in the footsteps of Hippolytus, Novatian became an antipope and caused a schism in the Roman church. Novatian sought recognition and validation of his illicit election from other Christian communities by sending letters to them announcing his "election." He also appointed loyal men as bishops and sent them throughout the Church. Novatian's schism lasted a few years until he was martyred during the persecution of Valerian.

Another group at odds with the bishops and the Church concerning the *lapsi* were the *laxists*, so called because they advocated for immediate readmittance of the *lapsi* without a period of penance. In his treatise on the *lapsi,* Cyprian expressed sharp words against this position:

> Their talk spreads like a canker, their conversation is catching as an infection, their poisonous and pernicious propaganda is more deadly than was the persecution itself. Those who do away with penance for sin, shut the door against satisfaction altogether. And so it is that, through the presumption of certain folk who beguile with false promises of salvation, all true hope of salvation is destroyed.[19]

The laxists were, perhaps, worse than the rigorists in that they led *lapsi* to believe they could be readmitted to the Church without any form of penance, thus depriving them of the ability to attain salvation. Excusing the sin without contrition and penitential satisfaction on the part of the sinner was akin to believing that apostasy was not even a sin. The rigorists and laxists held not only opposing views on the question about readmittance of the *lapsi*, but also produced disunity in the Church with their own leaders. Cyprian dealt with this problem in Carthage with the presence of Maximus the rigorist and Fortunatus the laxist, requiring attention he would have liked to give elsewhere.

Cyprian and other bishops spent the years after Decius's persecution ministering to their flock, combatting rigorists and laxists, and reconciling penitents. However, as rumors swirled concerning a possible persecution under the new emperor, Cyprian received a letter from six African bishops concerning the plight of three Christians who had lapsed during the prior persecution. These men had initially refused to sacrifice to the pagan gods, but after torture and in a physically weakened state, they gave in. The bishops argued that not all *lapsi*, especially those who gave in under duress, should be considered equal to those who willingly sacrificed. Cyprian agreed with this pastoral approach and stated that "such a plea may truly avail for forgiveness, such a defense deserves our pity."[20]

Under the threat of renewed persecution, Cyprian decided to hold another synod of bishops to re-evaluate the *lapsi* policy. Forty-two bishops attended the synod of 253, at which a recommendation about the *lapsi* was developed and communicated to Rome and other local churches. This synod allowed for the immediate readmittance of *sacrificati* no matter how many years of penance remained for them. The bishops made this change so that these Christians could be strengthened by grace from the Eucharist to hold fast during the impending persecution. Emperor Valerian initiated that persecution with an edict in 257 that specifically targeted the clergy. Pope St. Sixtus II (r. 257–258) was beheaded and his faithful deacon, St. Lawrence, was burned on a gridiron several days later. This time, Cyprian refused to leave Carthage and became the first African bishop martyred as a result of Valerian's edict. The Church suffered a few years under Valerian until he was captured in battle by the Persians, used as a stepstool by King Shapur I to mount his horse, and eventually died in captivity.

Just as the third century was a difficult time in Church history, so it was in imperial Roman history. The empire experienced profound political crisis as more than twenty emperors were murdered and a new emperor, on average, assumed the throne every three years. Diocles, who when he became emperor in 284 changed his name to Diocletian, was acutely aware of this instability and reorganized the empire's bureaucracy to address the problems. As part of the reorganization, Diocletian also created the *tetrarchy*—a political structure designed to provide a smooth transition of power upon the death of the emperor. The tetrarchy consisted of four rulers: two emperors (*Augusti*), one for each half of the empire, and two Caesars, who acted as deputies to the *Augusti*. Upon the death of an emperor, his Caesar became emperor and then appointed a new Caesar.

The system was designed to prevent the recurrent civil wars every time an emperor died.

Although initially tolerant of Christians, Diocletian was influenced by his Caesar, Galerius, in 303 to issue a series of repressive edicts designed to eradicate the Church from the empire. The edicts closed and confiscated all Christian churches and buildings, demanded the destruction of all copies of Scripture as well as sacred liturgical vessels, imprisoned, tortured, and executed the clergy, and in a final edict that mimicked Decius's general order in the previous century, required all Romans to sacrifice to the pagan gods. The *Great Persecution* was intense, especially in the eastern half of the empire, and the Church's roll of martyrs increased. As with the earlier Decian persecution, when the violence ended upon the death of Galerius in 311, the Church was faced with the question of the *lapsi,* but now it was well prepared to answer the pastoral questions. The bishop of Alexandria, Peter, issued several penal canons early in the fourth century concerning the *lapsi,* providing the length of penances required for various offenses. His canons reflect the earlier work of Sts. Cornelius and Cyprian in the mid-third century.

Renewal

After periods of imperial persecution, the Church was granted peace finally in the early fourth century, when the legions in Britain proclaimed Constantine, son of Constantius, the late Western Augustus, emperor, and unwittingly initiated a resurgence of the Faith. Constantine and his army marched through Gaul (modern-day France) on their way to battle with a rival claimant, Maxentius, in Rome, when they witnessed a miraculous vision. A cross, surrounded by the Latin phrase *In hoc signo vinces* ("In this sign, conquer") appeared in the sky. Believing it a positive omen from the Christian God signaling his victory in the upcoming campaign, Constantine ordered his troops to paint the *Chi Rho*, a Christian symbol, on their shields. When his army reached Rome, Constantine's troops won a stunning victory at the Battle of Milvian Bridge (October 28, 312) solidifying his claim to the western throne.

Constantine attributed his victory to the intercession of the Christian God and initiated a series of actions favoring the Catholic Church. The new Western emperor became a catechumen and issued edicts supporting the Church. Most famously, he signed, along with the Eastern emperor Licinius, the so-called Edict of Milan in 313, legalizing the Christian faith and allowing it universal toleration. Constantine also returned confiscated Christian property from the Great Persecution, provided the Church with new property (the Lateran palace), and appointed Christians to positions of imperial governance. But although Constantine viewed the Faith favorably and supported the Church, his motives were not entirely holy and spiritual. Political and temporal considerations were also important to him. Constantine desired to remain in power and viewed the Church as a means to ensure unity and peace in the empire. He became extremely agitated, therefore, when there was discord and disharmony in the Church. And despite the prior pastoral solutions concerning the *lapsi*, rigorist attitudes remained, especially in North Africa.

A group known as the Donatists caused Constantine agitation when they appealed to him for a ruling concerning two candidates for the episcopal see of Carthage. The Donatists desired their candidate, Donatus, over the duly and validly elected Caecilian, because they maintained that one of Caecilian's episcopal consecrators (a bishop named Felix) was a *lapsi*, although he had been cleared of any wrongdoing by a formal ecclesial inquiry. The Donatists held a rigorist view that the validity of a sacrament depends on the worthiness of the minister. Annoyed at the theological squabbling, Constantine eventually referred the matter to Pope St. Miltiades (r. 311–314), who decided in favor of Caecilian. However, the Donatists did not accept the pope's decision and appealed again to the emperor, who ruled against them.[21]

The rigorist-laxist debate was addressed in 325 at the first ecumenical council at Nicaea, called by Constantine to deal with the Christological heresy of the North African priest Arius. The bishops passed twenty canons at the council, of which five dealt with the *lapsi*. These canons provided the length of penance required for *lapsi* (twelve years for free-willed apostasy) and also contained merciful pastoral allowances, such as the ability for lapsed penitents to receive viaticum before the end of the penitential sentence, if warranted. The Nicene canons were rooted in the prior decisions of third-century bishops in the midst of active persecution and illustrated how the Church embraced Pope Cornelius and Cyprian's path of mercy and reconciliation of the *lapsi*.

In following centuries, the *exomologesis* of the early Church gave way to different methods of celebrating the sacrament of penance. A shift occurred from public penitential practices to private, and from proclamation of sin in the presence of the bishop to private auricular confession to a priest. (An echo of the *exomologesis* can be found in the Celtic Penitentials, books proscribing penances for various sins, of the early medieval period.)

The crisis of the lapsed thus brought about the renewal of the Church through an examination of the relationship of the sinner and the Church. The question of whether the Church, through the sacrament of confession, could pursue the path of authentic mercy between the rigorists and the laxists was definitively answered. The answer brought relief to the sinner and peace and unity to the Church and its members so greatly shaken by the violent persecutions of imperial Rome. Generations of Christians benefited from the thought, prayers, and work of holy bishops who ensured the Church would always be a school for sinners militantly pursuing holiness in order to spend eternity with God.

2

A Puppet Papacy

The Romans have found a singular means to palliate their insolent traffic in the election of popes. When they have made choice of a pontiff which it pleases them to raise to the Holy See, they strip him of his own name and give him the name of some great pope so that his want of merit will be obscured by the glory of his title.[22]

—Rodulfus Glaber

THE DARKNESS:
The collapse of Roman central governing authority in the late fifth century produced political upheaval in Europe. With the Church the only remaining international organization, powerful secular lords sought control of the papacy and maneuvered to place their own candidates

on the chair of St. Peter. This produced a series of weak, immoral, and incompetent popes and threatened irreparable harm to the Church.

THE LIGHT:
Ecclesial and secular reformers worked to free the papacy from secular control establishing sound and enduring papal election procedures.

Background

When central governing authority from Rome collapsed in the late fifth century, immense changes occurred in the Church and European society. Although the factors that led to the collapse of the imperial government had been centuries in the making, the immediate cause centered on the forced removal of the boy-emperor Romulus Augustulus by Odoacer the Hun. Romulus became emperor at the hands of his father, General Orestes. Odoacer, a commander of Roman auxiliary troops, demanded that Orestes give him a large swath of Italy to rule as his own. When Orestes refused, Odoacer marched his Huns to Rome, killed Orestes, and removed the sixteen-year-old Romulus from the throne. Odoacer declared himself king of Rome and reigned for nearly twenty years.

The collapse of central governing authority in the West resulted in a shift in the political and economic basis of society. Economically, the imperial bureaucracy—which collected taxes on land revenue—ceased to function and wealth instead became rooted in land holdings. Concurrently, those who had the manpower and wherewithal to accumulate and defend property grew in political clout. In the vacuum of central governance, ethnically German but Romanized local commanders of warriors exercised political power in small locales and regions, establishing the nascent foundation of European nobility that dominated the medieval and early modern periods. The Church in the Roman Empire was centered in urban areas and imperial administrative centers, and bishops, especially the bishop of Rome, became significant political players in a changing society dominated by various barbarian kingdoms.

Twenty years after Romulus's removal, Pope St. Gelasius I (r. 492–496) sent a letter to Anastastius I, the Eastern Roman emperor, describing the two powers in the world, spiritual and secular. The pope argued that the spiritual power is "more weighty" than the princely power because clerics have to "render an account for even the kings of men in the divine judgment."[23] The changing political dynamic heightened the Church's focus and role on temporal matters, which only increased further as centuries passed. As bishops became more involved in political affairs, the tension between Church and state increased and the understanding of the "two powers" and their interaction, articulated by Pope St. Gelasius I, changed.

As the Church entered the sixth century, it faced the task of converting the barbarian tribes now in power as a result of the imperial collapse. Many of these tribes embraced the

Arian heresy through the missionary efforts of the Arian bishop Ulfilas (311–383), some remained pagan, and a small minority professed the orthodox Catholic faith. Eventually, one major tribe, the Franks, converted to Catholicism through the prayers and encouragement of St. Clotilda (474–545), a Catholic Burgundian princess, who had married the Frankish king Clovis. Missionary efforts focused on the kings and chiefs of the various tribes because the contemporary worldview rooted the religion of a tribe in that of its ruler. St. Patrick (d. 461 or 493) achieved great success in Ireland pursuing this evangelization tactic as did St. Boniface (680–754), later in the eighth century, in German lands. St. Augustine of Canterbury, sent to England by Pope St. Gregory I the Great (r. 590–604), was successful in converting King Ethelbert of Kent, which ensured the permanence of the Faith in that land.

The emergence of Islam in the seventh century and its subsequent expansion and conquest of ancient Christian territory altered the relationship of the Church with the Eastern Roman Empire.[24] Islamic conquests in the Holy Land, North Africa, and Spain, as well as large raids into modern-day France and Italy, including Rome, in the eighth and ninth centuries, turned the Church's attention northward to the Continent and away from the east and Mediterranean. The eruption in the East of the Iconoclast heresy, which forbade sacred images, also impacted relations between the two halves of the empire. The popes turned to secular rulers closer to Italy for sources of political and military support, and, in the eighth century, settled on the rulers of the Franks, the inheritors of Clovis.

The Merovingian "shadow kings" of the Franks were weak and exercised limited authority in the realm. It was the mayors of the palace (essentially, supreme commanders of the military and prime ministers of royal government), who instead wielded influence and power. In the mid-eighth century, a mayor of the palace named Pepin, son of the famous Charles Martel who had stopped an Islamic raiding force at Poitiers in 732, asked Pope St. Zachary (r. 741–752) who should reign as king: one who actually exercised power or one who held authority in name only? The pope replied that the one who exercised power should be king, which gave Pepin legitimacy in removing the last Merovingian king from the throne and establishing a new dynasty. Later, Pope Stephen III (r. 752–757) traveled to Francia and named Pepin and his sons, Carolman and Charles, protectors of the Romans. When the Lombards—an ethnically Germanic people who originally migrated to northern Italy in the middle of the sixth century—threatened Rome, Pepin and his Frankish warriors marched to Italy to defend the papacy. The subsequent campaign ended in the defeat of the Lombards and the granting of captured territory by Pepin to the pope as his own patrimony. The creation of the *Papal States*, the pope's personal land holdings in northern and central Italy, resulted in a new era for the papacy marked by increased mixture of temporal and spiritual concerns.

Papal relationships with secular rulers entered a new phase in the year 800 when Pope St. Leo III (r. 795–816) crowned Charlemagne, son of Pepin, as emperor. The previous year, Leo had been attacked as he led a liturgical procession through the streets, by a mob upset with his election due to wild accusations against him. When news of the harassment reached Charlemagne, he was incensed. Leo fled Rome for Francia to meet with the king, who sent him back to Rome with an armed Frankish escort and promises to travel to Rome in the near future. Charlemagne arrived in the Eternal City at the end of the year and attended a gathering assembled to clear Leo's name. The pope proclaimed his innocence of the charges and, at the same assembly, the nobles and clergy encouraged Charlemagne to assume the title of emperor. Charlemagne's reputation was well known and he ruled over a vast territory; additionally, there was no emperor in the East, only an empress (Irene). On Christmas Day, to much acclaim from the assembled people, Pope Leo crowned Charlemagne emperor.

With this act, Leo made permanent the papacy's linkage with the Frankish kings and broke the influence of the Eastern emperor in the West, which had been waning for decades. Furthermore, Leo established the procedure of papal coronation of emperors. The imperial title was now tied to the papacy; it was not inherited and was not automatic but had to be papally conferred. This increased the power of the Church—but it also embroiled the papacy in temporal political and military affairs for centuries and was a major factor in the crisis in the papacy that marked the ninth, tenth, and eleventh centuries.

Crisis

Christendom in the ninth and tenth centuries was witness to violent struggles that led to depopulation, agricultural problems, and societal instability. Islamic raids throughout the Mediterranean and in Italy continued. The Magyars, a nomadic people, invaded Italy at the end of the ninth century and wreaked havoc throughout central Europe in the tenth. A battlefield defeat in the mid-tenth century and their subsequent conversion to the Catholic faith finally pacified these violent ancestors of modern-day Hungarians. Pagan Norsemen ravaged England and France during the ninth century. English kings initially dealt with the piratical marauders through bribes, known as *danegeld*, but the Vikings wanted land as well as booty. Viking warriors attacked Paris in the mid-ninth century, sailing up the Seine with over a hundred ships and constructing siege towers in order to get into the city. Hardly any major city was immune to the plundering, destruction, and death wrought by the Vikings (though some groups settled in England and northern France and established stable political entities). Even after their conversion, it was difficult for Norsemen to fully embrace the Faith, as evidenced by Viking gravestones from the late medieval period that bear Christian symbols on one side as well as Wotan and other pagan deities on the other.[25]

While Christendom was suffering the ravages of Muslim, Magyar, and Viking warriors during the ninth century, the papacy suffered from incompetent popes controlled by local Roman aristocratic families. The lone exception was Pope

St. Nicholas I the Great (r. 858–867), who strongly and successfully asserted the moral, political, and ecclesial authority of the successor of St. Peter. He rebuked Lothair, king of Lorraine, for his illegitimate relationship with a concubine and the divorce of his wife Theutberga. When the layman Photius was appointed patriarch of Constantinople illegitimately, Nicholas refused papal recognition even in the midst of threats from the Eastern emperor Michael III (affectionally known in history as "the Drunkard").

With the death of Pope Nicholas in 867, the papacy entered into a dark chapter in its history, illustrated by the presence of only two papal saints, Nicholas I and Adrian III (r. 884–885) from 867 to 1042—a timeline of 182 years and forty-four popes! The papacy was not only absent saintliness in its occupants but also was witness to high crimes, scandal, and macabre events. No fewer than twelve pontiffs from the late ninth through the mid-eleventh century were murdered—poisoned, strangled, suffocated, or bludgeoned—or died under mysterious circumstances. The papacy became a dangerous place due to the machinations of local noble Italian families and other regional rulers who vied to control the important position.

This "game of thrones" environment is best illustrated in the five-year pontificate of Pope Formosus (r. 891–896) at the end of the ninth century. Formosus was a well-known churchman and a contentious figure in Christendom before his papal election. Once pope, Formosus became embroiled in the political question concerning the holy roman emperor.

In 891, Pope Stephen VI (r. 885–891) crowned one Guy of Spoleto, a ferocious warlord with a band of Muslim mercenaries at his disposal. He was also the brother of Lambert I of Spoleto, who had looted Rome in 878. Despite his coronation as emperor, there were other warlords who laid claim to the imperial title. Formosus backed different men at different times depending on the political situation. Early in his pontificate he had crowned Lambert II of Spoleto, Guy's son, as co-emperor but also supported Arnulf, Duke of Carinthia (in modern-day Austria). Berengar of Friuli (in northeastern Italy), a descendant of Charlemagne, also sought the pope's approval. Formosus favored Arnulf and Berengar because of their distance from Rome but also placated Guy and Lambert II. Eventually, Formosus shunned them for Arnulf, who invaded Italy with a large army. Formosus's troubles only ended when he died on Easter Sunday 896 at the age of eighty.

The next pope, Boniface VI, reigned for two weeks only before his death and was replaced by Stephen VII (r. 896–897). Stephen's short pontificate was witness to one of the most ghoulish scenes in Church history. Angry at the behavior of Pope Formosus over the imperial title, the spurned Lambert II of Spoleto entered Rome in 897 and demanded Stephen VII place his deceased predecessor on trial for alleged violations of canon law. Sadly, the pope agreed to Lambert's macabre demands. The corpse of Pope Formosus was exhumed, dressed in pontifical robes with his hair shirt underneath and propped up in a seat for the trial. Since the dead pontiff could not speak in his defense, the corpse was provided a deacon to serve as defense lawyer. Although the deacon likely tried his best, the task proved futile as the "Synod of the Corpse" ended in a guilty verdict for Pope Formosus.

The corpse's pontifical robes were stripped off, three fingers of the right hand were severed, and the body was dragged through the church and thrown into a grave. (Robbers later dug up the corpse and threw it into the Tiber.) A few months later, Pope Stephen VII met his ignoble end when strangled. The next two popes reigned for short periods (four months for Romanus and twenty days for Theodore II) but then John IX (r. 898–900) was elected and annulled and condemned Stephen's actions.

The troubles in the ninth-century papacy later gave rise to a fanciful papal myth that still finds adherents in the modern world. The myth, first recorded in the thirteenth century, tells the story of a female pope (the infamous "Pope Joan"), who hid her sex by dressing as a man.[26] Joan was educated and found employment as a teacher in Rome (another version of the story has her working as a papal bureaucrat). Eventually, her talents were recognized by the Church and she was "elected" pope by the unknowing Roman clergy. Joan's secret was revealed when she gave birth, after hiding her pregnancy, during a liturgical procession through the streets of the Eternal City. One version of the myth indicates that Joan died as a result of childbirth, but a more dramatic version tells of an enraged mob tying her to a horse that dragged her through the streets and ends in a stoning.[27] Although historically false, the legend of "Pope Joan" does illuminate the sad state of affairs in the ninth-century papacy.

Unfortunately, the following century did not improve the political and ecclesial troubles in Christendom, as evidenced by this description from the Synod of Trosly (in modern-day northern France):

> The towns are depopulated, the monasteries ruined and burned; the good land turned into desert. Just as primitive man lived without law, and without fear of God, giving himself up wholly to his passions, so today everyone does what seems good in his own sight, in defiance of human and divine laws and the commandments of the Church; the strong oppress the weak; the world is filled with violence toward the young and unprotected; and men steal the goods which belong to the Church. Men devour one another like the fishes of the sea.[28]

Tenth-century Europe witnessed political instability, societal upheaval, and the creation of powerful military lords who built castles to control territory. When Berengar of Friuli died in 924, after a reign of thirty-six years that witnessed multiple rival claimants, the imperial title lapsed for nearly a generation as popes refused to anoint an emperor due to political squabbles with various secular lords. The tenth-century papacy became the plaything of secular rulers, as the See of St. Peter lost its independence and became a seat of immorality, corruption, and such sinful behavior that Cardinal Baronius, the sixteenth-century Church historian, referred to this time period as a "pornocracy."[29] A wealthy and powerful Tuscan family controlled the papacy for more than half of the tenth century. Known as the *Theophylacts* for the patriarch who was a mighty soldier as well as in charge of the papal treasury, the family, under the tutelage of Theodora (wife of Theophylact) and Marozia (a daughter), dominated papal politics and elections.

The family's influence reached its zenith in the pontificate of John XII (r. 955–963), who was the great-grandson of Theophylact and Theodora. On his deathbed, Duke Alberic II of Spoleto (grandson of the power couple) forced his nobles to swear an oath to make his son, Octavian, pope, when the opportunity presented itself. When Pope Agapetus II (r. 946–955) died, the nobles complied and elevated Octavian to the Chair of St. Peter. A young man (sources indicate sixteen or eighteen years old), Octavian decided to take a papal name and was known as John XII (r. 955–963); theretofore, only one other pope (John II in 533) had changed his name upon election.[30] The young pope focused his attention on carnal pleasures, turning the papal palace into a veritable brothel. John XII enjoyed hunting, gambling, and sexual adventures with numerous women, and pursued a papal agenda of "deliberate sacrilege that went far beyond the casual enjoyment of sensual pleasure."[31] Apparently extremely jealous as well, John allegedly had one cleric castrated because he bedded a former papal mistress.[32] Besides his sexual proclivities, John engaged in ecclesiastical abuses such as *simony*—the buying and selling of ecclesial offices.[33]

Perhaps the one bright spot in a very dark papacy was John's invitation to Otto, king of the Germans, to come to Rome to protect him against a powerful noble. Otto was the son of Henry I, the "Fowler," king of Germans (r. 919–936) and a devoted Catholic who attended Mass daily. Otto eagerly came to the pope's aid and in return John crowned him emperor in 962, restoring the imperial title after an interregnum of thirty-eight years. This action solidified the imperial title with the rulers of German territory for centuries, producing a complex relationship between popes and secular rulers. John XII died the next year—allegedly of a stroke while in bed with a married woman.

The tenth century produced no papal saints. The early eleventh-century papacy continued the string of incompetent, corrupt, and worldly pontiffs. The death of Pope Sergius IV in 1012, after a three-year-long papacy, produced a literal street fight between two rival Italian families, the Crescenzi and the Theophylacts (again). The Crescenzi family candidate (Gregory) won the street fight but the Theophylact candidate (Benedict) sought the intervention of Henry II, king of the Germans, whose support produced the desired outcome. Benedict VIII (r. 1012–1024) became pope (Gregory became an antipope) and, in exchange, bestowed the imperial title on Henry in 1014. This papal and imperial arrangement actually benefited the Church, as

Benedict VIII and Henry II sought to reform the Church. At the synod of Pavia in 1022, the pope, with imperial backing, issued a number of reform canons aimed at eradicating simony and enforcing clerical celibacy. Unfortunately, both men died shortly thereafter (in 1024) so the reform decrees were not successfully implemented.[34]

The papacy remained in the Theophylact family with the election of John XIX (r. 1024–1032), Benedict VIII's brother, and another Theophylact family member became pope upon John XIX's death. Nephew of the previous two popes, Benedict IX (r. 1032–1045; 1045; 1047–1048) represents a unique distinction in the line of the popes: he is the only man to appear as a successor of St. Peter more than once. Benedict IX's pontificate was also the epitome of the immoral and corrupt papacies of the age. He committed the crime of simony by using a substantial sum of money, provided by his father Count Alberic III, to secure his election at only twenty years old, and lived such a debauched lifestyle as pope that the Roman populace tired of his wickedness and forced him from the city in 1044. Sylvester III, an antipope, was elected and "reigned" for less than two months before Benedict triumphantly returned to the city. However, Benedict IX tired of the papacy and its demands, and perhaps desirous of marriage (allegedly to his cousin), he resigned the papacy on March 1, 1045. Before his resignation, in 1032, Benedict demanded reimbursement of the money utilized to secure the papacy. John Gratian, a priest and Benedict's godfather, raised the large sum and repaid

Benedict. John was then elected pope taking the name
Gregory VI (r. 1045–1046).

Despite his holy reputation and backing by reform-
minded clerics, Gregory VI too committed simony in order
to secure the Chair of St. Peter. News of this crime became
public knowledge and support for his pontificate waned.
Additionally, Benedict IX regretted his decision to resign,
returned to Rome in 1046, and demanded reinstatement.
The debacle of three men claiming the papacy (Benedict
IX, Gregory VI, and the antipope Sylvester III) forced secular intervention by Henry III, king of the Germans, son of
the previous emperor Conrad II who died in 1039.

Henry III decided to settle the papal question at a synod
in the town of Sutri (about an hour's drive northwest of
Rome) in December 1046. The king ordered Gregory VI,
Benedict IX, and Sylvester III to attend the synod but only
Gregory appeared. Recognizing his simony, Gregory VI
consented to resign the papacy. Benedict IX's request to
reclaim the papacy was denied and antipope Sylvester III was
condemned and ordered to a monastery. Henry III nominated a new pope, the German bishop Sudiger of Bamberg,
who was elected by the Roman clergy and acclaimed by the
people and took the name Clement II (r. 1046–1047). The
newly consecrated pope crowned Henry III (r. 1046–1056)
emperor on Christmas Day 1046. The strange saga of Benedict IX was not over, however, as he refused to recognize
the outcome at Sutri. Upon the death of Clement II in 1047,
Benedict IX returned to Rome to resume the papacy. His

final "term" as pope was cut short when he was forced out of Rome (again) and replaced by another German bishop, who took the name Damasus II (r. 1048).

By the mid-eleventh century, it was clear to many within the Church that changes were needed. Although simony and clerical marriage/concubinage were significant problems, papal incompetence, worldliness, and corruption hindered reform. Bishops and secular lords did address many issues on a local level, but universal implementation was lacking. Church reformers, both clerical and lay, recognized the need to liberate the papacy from secular interference, especially from the clutches of local Italian noble families such as the Theophylacts. As a result, the method of papal elections became a main issue.

Renewal

In the early Church, papal elections were administered by the clergy and people of Rome but there was no specified method. This approach served the needs of the Church for centuries, but the collapse of central imperial governing authority from Rome at the end of the fifth century and the political instability in the subsequent centuries culminated in an untenable situation that produced the debacle of Benedict IX's pontificate(s). The constant infighting and intrigue weakened the papacy's effectiveness and stature.

The aftermath of the Synod of Sutri and the return of Benedict IX convinced Holy Roman Emperor Henry III that, for the good of the Church, he needed to remain involved in the papal election process. So, for the next decade he nominated for the papacy a series of German bishops known for their reforming zeal. These bishops took papal names with historical pedigree: Clement, Damasus, and Leo.[35] Henry believed that a process of imperial nomination of a candidate followed by formal election by the Roman clergy and acclamation by the Roman populace would bring stability to the papacy and free it from the squabbling and clutches of Italian families. This imperially focused method worked for a time, but it had a fundamental flaw: reliance on the emperor's whim. In the hands of a pious and devoted emperor, this method could produce excellent papal candidates, but in the hands of a self-serving secular ruler, the potential for ecclesial disaster was high. This is one reason why the method of papal election was changed in 1059.

Meddling in papal elections returned in 1058 when Stephen X (r. 1057–1058) died. One powerful family forced its candidate, Benedict X, onto the Chair of St. Peter but a group of reformers meeting in Siena elected Nicholas II (r. 1058–1061), who entered Rome, excommunicated Benedict X, and strengthened his political position by entering into alliances with Norman warlords in southern Italy. In an attempt to bring stability to papal succession and solidify control of papal elections within the clergy, St. Peter Damian (1007–1072) proposed, in 1057, the idea of cardinal-bishops electing the pope. Championed by the papal adviser Hildebrand (the future Pope St. Gregory VII), the idea intrigued Pope Nicholas. Originally, cardinals had served at liturgical functions at the Lateran and other Roman churches and were grouped into three categories of *cardinal-deacons*, *cardinal-priests*, and *cardinal-bishops*. Cardinal-deacons performed liturgical and administrative tasks along with various pastoral duties, cardinal-priests were assigned to titular churches in Rome, and cardinal-bishops presided over the seven suburbicarian sees (Ostia, Palestrina, Porto, Albano, Silva-Candida, Velletri, and Labiacum) near Rome. Three cardinal-bishops held the traditional role of consecrating a new pope once elected and all cardinal-bishops were assigned a weekly rotation of liturgical duties at the Lateran. Peter Damian and Hildebrand believed that having cardinals elect the pope would ensure papal independence from the meddlesome influence of secular rulers.

Pope Nicholas convoked a synod in Rome in the spring of 1059 to discuss the issue. The result was the *Decree on Papal Elections* promulgated on April 14, 1059, with the assent of more than a hundred assembled bishops. The *Decree* stipulated that at the death of a pope, the cardinal-bishops were to gather and elect a successor from the Church in Rome or elsewhere.[36] The other cardinals and clergy of Rome maintained a role in the election as well as the people of Rome, whose consent was still required. No specific voting majority was stipulated in the *Decree*, but the later Third Lateran Council (1179) modified the papal election process by requiring a two-thirds majority for the successful candidate.

The reform decree of Pope Nicholas II was a watershed moment in Church history. His action disentangled the papacy from secular control and greatly elevated the importance of the cardinals and their role in the Church. Although in future centuries the method suffered from problems, such as national rivalries among the cardinals that prevented agreement on candidates, which produced long papal interregnums, it remains the method of papal election to this day, nearly a thousand years later—proving its brilliance and resiliency. The new process assisted in producing reform-minded popes through the remaining years of the century and for several hundred years more freed the Church from disruptive and inappropriate secular interference in the papacy. Nicholas's decree rooted the method of choosing a pope within the Church, but it would not have developed without the crises in the papacy during the nineth, tenth, and eleventh centuries.

3
———

Clerical Corruption and Sexual Immorality

But what a criminal situation! Shamelessly this epidemic has been so audaciously revealed that everyone knows the houses of prostitution, the fathers-in-law . . . and other close relatives . . . and lastly to remove all doubt, you have the obvious pregnancies and the squalling babies.[37]

—St. Peter Damian

THE DARKNESS:
In the late eleventh century, the evils of clerical corruption and sexual immorality plagued the Church extensively, weakening the influence of the gospel and obstructing the Church's salvific mission.

THE LIGHT:
God brought forth a stalwart defender of purity and truth who exhorted the pope to reform the clergy. The monastic reform produced holy men later elected to the papacy who initiated one of the most comprehensive ecclesial reforms in history.

Background

As the Church entered the eleventh century, the discipline of clerical celibacy in the West was well established. The promise of celibacy, freely taken, dates to the early Church and is rooted in theology and early Christian living, although its application changed and developed over time. In the first three centuries of Church history, there had been no law prohibiting the ordination of married men, and priests were frequently married; however, marriage was never permitted after ordination, and all men, whether married, single, or widowed, practiced sexual abstinence after ordination to the priesthood. The writings of the Church Fathers Tertullian (163–230), Origen (185–254), Eusebius of Caesarea (260–341) and St. Epiphanius (310–403) attest to the practice of clerical celibacy in the early centuries of the Church.

The first recorded Church legislation mandating the rule of celibacy for clergy in the West occurred at the Synod of Elvira in Spain around the year 300,[38] and universal application of the discipline received papal legislation in the late fourth century during the pontificate of Pope St. Siricius (r. 384–399). At a synod of bishops in February 385, the pope issued a *decretal*, modeled after imperial decretals that responded to questions asked of the emperor, indicating that clerical celibacy was an unbreakable rule without exceptions. Violations of the practice entailed ecclesiastical penalties with deposition reserved to the apostolic see. At a council in Rome nearly a year later (January 386), the pope ruled that celibacy was required of all clergy. Even though the early Church had permitted the ordination of married men, virginity for the sake of the kingdom of heaven was highly regarded. Celibacy was practiced by men who left the world to seek closer union with God in the desert and monasteries. Christian women, both consecrated virgins and widows, pledged celibacy out of love for God in large numbers in the early Church. At the time of St. John Chrysostom (c. 347–407), there were 3,000 virgins and widows in the great city of Constantinople.[39]

Although a mandated practice, clerical celibacy was not always lived authentically as clerics gave into the temptations of the flesh. By the eleventh century, many clerics throughout Christendom were living openly with women and their children. Infidelity to the promise of celibacy also resulted in the pervasive practice of homosexuality within monasteries and posed a significant problem for the Church in the medieval period.

By the middle of the eleventh century, clerical infidelity to celibacy (along with simony) drew the ire of holy monks who desired a return to authentic Christian living on the part of the clergy. When these monks were elected to the papacy, they initiated one of the most comprehensive reforms in Church history.

Crisis

In order to eradicate abuses and corruption, they must be exposed. The man most famous for exposing the darkness of clerical sexual immorality and the abhorrent practice of simony in the eleventh century was St. Peter Damian (1007–1072). Born in Ravenna, Peter suffered immense tragedy in his early life. The death of his parents when he was an infant resulted in his relocation to live with an older brother. The brother and his concubine raised Peter in an abusive home where he was starved, beaten, and, when old enough, sent to work as a swineherd. Peter's sanctity was observed at an early age and fostered by another brother, Damian, who rescued him from the clutches of abuse. Damian loved Peter and ensured his education in the liberal arts. Grateful for his brother's love and support, Peter took his name and was henceforth known as Peter Damian.[40] His bright mind and diligent studies brought Peter attention so that he was soon enlisted to teach others. Peter taught for a few years but, at the age of twenty-eight, disillusioned with the world and its vices, he joined the hermitage at Fonte-Avellana (about 150 miles northeast of Rome).

Committed to holy and virtuous living, Peter focused on personal sanctity initially but then turned his attention to reform within the hermitage and then later to the secular (diocesan) clergy and society as a whole. Although ensconced in the hermitage, Peter kept abreast of events in the Church and world and wrote letters to popes and bishops concerning the state of the Church and the need for reform. The abuses of simony and clerical sexual immorality drew his attention, and in 1049 he began writing what came to be called the *Liber Gomorrhianus* (*Book of Gomorrah*). The work, dedicated to Pope St. Leo IX (r. 1049–1054), is an exhortation to the pope to root out the evil of sexual sins, including homosexuality and the taking of mistresses, from the clergy throughout the Church. Peter shed light on the rampant sexual sins of the clergy, calling them a "diabolical tyranny" that produced a "cancer of sodomitic impurity."[41] He remarked that these sins were "raging like a cruel beast within the sheepfold of Christ" and believed that unless the pope "opposes it as quickly as possible, there is no doubt that when [he] finally wishes for the unbridled evil to be restrained, [he] may not be able to halt the fury of its advance."[42]

Peter condemned clerical sexual immorality in still-starker language, calling those who engaged in homosexual acts "degenerate men [who] do not fear to perpetuate an act that even brute animals abhor. That which is done by the temerity of human depravity is condemned by the judgment of irrational cattle."[43] Peter addressed a multitude of sexual sins in his polemic to the pope, including contraception, masturbation, pederasty, and adult homosexual activity, and underscored the severe penalties imposed for these sins in Scripture as well as ecclesial legislation.[44] Peter advocated that those with homosexual tendencies should not be ordained and called for severe penalties for priests who absolve in the confessional penitents they had abused. However, Peter did not merely condemn the sexual sins of the clergy but expressed deep compassion for those who had fallen and expressed a fervent desire for their conversion and reconciliation to God and the Church. He advised brother priests who struggled with sexual sins and were tempted by the devil to "immediately turn [your] eyes to the graves of the dead."[45]

The pope responded favorably to Peter's treatise on clerical sexual immorality, praising him for the courage to raise "the arm of the Spirit against the obscenity of lust" and noting the hermit's virtue in practicing the chastity he expected of his fellow clerics.[46]

Along with other religious and secular reformers, notably Humbert of Moyenmoutier (who wrote a work titled *Against Simony* in 1057), Peter also turned his holy attention to the crime of simony. A few years after his work against clerical sexual immorality, the righteous hermit penned his *Liber Gratissimus* (*Most Gracious Book*). Simony was so extensive in the Church in the eleventh century that the majority of bishops in Christendom were guilty of the nefarious deed.[47] Peter surveyed the clerical landscape of his time and remarked, "the custom of simony was so widespread that hardly anyone knew it was a sin."[48] The abuse raised the concern of secular rulers and ecclesiastics who held local councils to discuss the issue. The abuse was of grave concern because it rooted priestly ordination in greed and made clerics susceptible to secular control. Peter was so incensed at the sin he discussed it in frank language: "hardly any festering wound causes a more intolerable stench for the nose of God than the excrement that is greed."[49] Unlike some reformers, Peter did not adhere to the conviction that those who were guilty of simony held invalid ordinations. This erroneous belief was akin to the Donatist heresy in the early Church that posited the validity of a sacrament depended on the worthiness of the minister.

Pope Stephen X (r. 1057–1058) created Peter cardinal, despite his reluctance and initial refusal of the distinction. Other popes sent Peter on various legatine missions throughout Christendom. He died in 1072 on the homeward journey from a special mission to Ravenna (his birthplace). Although St. Peter Damian highlighted the need for reform in the Church from the vices of simony and clerical simony, his oratory required strong papal leadership and the implementation of a reform plan for change to occur.

Renewal

The papal reform initiative of the eleventh century came in the wake of the abuses witnessed in the papacy and the degradation of clerical behavior in the ninth through eleventh centuries. The reform was a series of events and initiatives undertaken locally and universally over years, not always hierarchically coordinated, and varied in approach from pope to pope.[50] The language utilized by those who desired an eradication of the abuses within the Church and secular interference from without indicates the perspective of the holy initiatives. Words such as *renewal, renovation,* and *restoration* were more often chosen in works describing the initiatives rather than *reform.*[51] Clerics tired of the sins of their fellow clergy and angry at secular control of the Church, especially the papacy, viewed their actions as a restoration of the pristine nature and constitution of the Church, not as a change or modification. They wanted a return to what they saw as the golden age in Church history—a time from the fourth through sixth centuries when secular rulers respected, guarded, and worked in cooperation with the Church rather than seeking to subjugate it.

Of course, this idyllic situation did not actually exist in those centuries, but the reformers viewed them more favorably than the "iron age" in which they lived, where laymen controlled the Church, took its property, and blurred the distinction between the secular and the spiritual.[52]

The goal of the reform movement was thus twofold: liberate the Church from undue secular interference and enforce clerical discipline by eradicating the twin abuses of simony and clerical sexual immorality. Bl. Pope Urban II (r. 1088–1099) articulated the main focus of the movement when he wrote that "the Church shall be Catholic, chaste and free: Catholic in the faith and fellowship of the saints, chaste from all contagion of evil, and free from secular power."[53] The impetus of the reform movement came from monks living in reformed monasteries, faithful to their founder and rule, who were elevated to the papacy.[54] These were men free from the sins of simony, corruption, and unchastity and had the holy desire to renew the Church and restore its clergy.

The antecedent of the eleventh-century papal reform movement centered, in part, on ending the bloodshed between Christians in parts of Christendom. The so-called "Peace of God" (tenth century) and "Truce of God" (eleventh century) movements in France and German territory involved more than crafting rules and regulations of warfare between Christians. The movement really focused on land issues and the protection of the landless populace as well as the Church.[55] In the post-Carolingian world of the tenth century, European society saw a shift in hereditary rights of land. Carolingian society had followed the Frankish custom of dividing territory among the surviving sons of a ruler, but that tradition gave way to the new practice of *primogeniture* or primary inheritance to the firstborn son. Additionally, secular rulers gifted land to the Church as a benefice for the life of the benefactor, which produced instability when the benefactor died and his heir decided to withdraw the benefice or change its terms. The Church, seeking greater stability, desired land gifts in perpetuity.

Bishops in tenth-century France, at times in association with local lords, convoked large outdoor meetings to discuss the problem of secular lords pillaging churches and attacking the poor. The bishops threatened the perpetrators with excommunication and required warriors to take an oath for the maintenance of peace and the protection of clerics, the poor, and the weak. The assemblies became popular meetings that even included the presence of relics. Although initially concerned with peace and security issues, the meetings began to address other issues of concern for the Church, including the banning of clerics from bearing arms or accepting money or gifts for the celebration of the sacraments, and abuses such as simony, heresy, and sexual immorality in clerics and the laity.[56] These assemblies provided a foundation of ecclesial and secular cooperation in the eradication of abuses and immorality that threatened the stability, unity, and peace of medieval Christian society. Although the "Peace of God" and "Truce of God" movements offered opportunities and a format for reform in the Church and society, they were local affairs. A universal application of their reforming nature required universal leadership and implementation.

And that leadership for the Church-wide reform program was provided by Bruno of Alsace, who as Pope St. Leo IX (r. 1049–1054), advanced one of the most comprehensive ecclesial reform agendas in history.

Bruno was born into a noble and holy family. He began a career in the Church, and his abilities along with his personal piety were soon recognized. Eventually, he was consecrated bishop of Toul (in modern-day northeastern France), where he became known for his commitment to reform and renewal. He served as bishop of Toul for more than twenty years and was content to remain until his life was altered radically by the Holy Roman Emperor Henry

III. At an imperial assembly at Worms in December 1048, the emperor nominated Bruno to assume the duties of the bishop of Rome upon the death of Pope Damasus II. Bruno did not accept the nomination, citing his unsuitability for the office. He reflected for three days on the actions of the emperor, God's will, and his future. Eventually, Bruno accepted the challenge and traveled to Rome. However, he stressed he would not assume the papal office unless unanimously elected by the clergy and people, which occurred. The new pope was crowned on February 12, 1049.

Taking the name Leo IX, Bruno focused on three major issues during his pontificate: Church reform, the protection of the Papal States from the Normans, and the resolution of disputes with the Byzantines.[57] Leo IX thus launched one of the most comprehensive reforms in Church history and did so with great zeal, making the papacy an active participant rather than a bystander in the reform efforts of the eleventh century. Leo brought ecclesial reformers from the north to Rome, including Humbert of Moyenmoutier (who was created cardinal-bishop of Silva-Candida in 1050), and Frederick of Lorraine, the future Pope Stephen X, to assist in his reform efforts. He began his renewal with a synod in Rome in the year 1049, only six weeks after his consecration wherein the evil vices of simony and violations of clerical celibacy were condemned. Notorious prelates guilty of simony were placed on trial. One guilty cleric, the bishop of Sutri, dropped dead of a heart attack at Leo's feet while arguing his innocence![58]

A year later at another synod in Rome, Leo issued an excommunication for all clerics publicly living in violation of their promise of celibacy. Leo recognized that authentic reform could not be simply mandated from afar but must be implemented locally, so he traveled throughout Italy, German territories, and France holding twelve total reform synods. Leo's focus on reform and renewal was so intense that he spent only six months of his five-and-a-half-year pontificate in Rome due to traveling to and from various synods. Many local bishops embraced the papal initiative and conducted their own diocesan synods to enforce the papal reform program. In his inaugural papal year, Leo traveled to Reims in France to consecrate a new basilica at the shrine of St. Remy (437–533) and also conducted a three-day synod to enforce his reform decrees. On the first day of the synod, all bishops and abbots were required to take an oath that their ecclesial office was free from the stain of simony. Leo spent the next three days of the synod examining and judging those clerics held in suspicion of simony. Wherever he went, Pope Leo IX deposed immoral bishops and punished clerics engaged in simony, infidelity, and violations of chastity.

Reaction among the clergy to Leo's reform efforts was mixed. As the English Benedictine chronicler Orderic Vitalis recorded: "Clerics were ready enough to give up bearing arms, but even now were loath to part with their mistresses or to live chaste lives."[59]

Leo's reform initiatives were impeded somewhat by distractions from the Norman invasion of southern Italy and a theological tiff with Eastern Christians in Constantinople. However, the eleventh-century papal reform movement resulted in a renewal of clerical life that could scarcely have been imagined a century earlier when abuse was so rampant. Monks from reformed monasteries faithful to the spiritual vision of their founders led the movement and were able to initiate universal implementation when elected to the papacy.

Reformers desired also a Church free from the influence of secular authority, in which clerics were more loyal to the Faith than to their temporal lords. That reorientation of loyalties in medieval society came toward the end of the century from the actions of another pope and eventually resulted in the establishment of clear boundaries between secular and spiritual spheres. Although the eradication of personal sin is a personal struggle, the Church's pastors have the task of laying out standards of virtuous clerical living and appointments to clerical offices. The reformer monk-popes of the eleventh century accomplished those tasks and provided a sure foundation for proper clerical behavior for centuries to come.

4

The Investiture Controversy

We decree that no one of the clergy shall receive the investiture with a bishopric or abbey or church from the hand of an emperor or king or of any lay person, male or female. But if shall presume to do so he shall clearly know that such investiture is bereft of apostolic authority, and that he himself shall lie under excommunication until fitting satisfaction shall have been rendered.[60]

—Pope St. Gregory VII

THE DARKNESS:
Secular interference in the Church continued, especially in German lands, where the king invested bishops with the symbols of their Church office and secular office and so divided their loyalties.

THE LIGHT:
Reformers fought the practice of lay investiture and eventually the pope banned the practice, leading to a compromise that recognized the Church's distinct sphere of authority.

Background

In the ninth and tenth centuries, European society found itself completely transformed by the disintegration of Carolingian political structures and buckling under near-constant attacks from Vikings, Magyars, and Muslims. The need for protection from invaders created a dichotomy in society between those who could provide security and those who needed it. An "oligarchy of warriors" thus developed in which protection was provided but at a price: the price of "subordination, subjection, and dependence."[61] What became known by later historians as "medieval society" embraced a system of societal structures rooted in landholding and personal relationships given the name *feudalism*.[62]

According to the standard narrative, feudalism "denote[d] the grant of income-producing property (usually land), known as the benefice or fief, by the lord and protector in return for the promise of oath of fealty by the vassal."[63] Prior to the tenth century, land was *allodial* or free from conditions, but with the changing political conditions, certain warriors came to control large areas of land and, in order to administer them properly, decided to parcel land to other warriors in exchange for military assistance and a percentage of the fruits of the property. In the old imperial Roman days, the basis of the economy was taxes but in the post-Carolingian world, landholding determined wealth. Over time, therefore, questions of *inheritance* dominated the minds of the clergy and nobility. Initially, land was granted for the life of the benefactor, but the Church encouraged inheritable fiefs in an effort to promote greater societal and ecclesial stability. This change prevented the renegotiation of terms or the loss of land upon the death of benefactor and contributed to the Church's growth in status and power in society. "Feudalism" was not a perfect system, nor was it uniformly practiced throughout Christendom; indeed, it was mostly used in the areas of modern-day France and England.[64]

Medieval society was rooted in personal relationships, and the most important relationship was between a lord and his vassal/subject. Their relationship centered on the exchange of duties and responsibilities and was entered into by an oath.[65] Initially known as *commendation* and later as *homage*, the oath bound one man to another. The lord promised protection and land or money in exchange for military service (before the twelfth century, this was true only in England), counsel, and aid. *Fealty*, or the promise of faithfulness, was only performed by the vassal or subject to the lord. It was possible to pledge fealty without homage but not homage without fealty.[66] Once the oath was provided, the lord would *invest* the vassal with the benefice or fief in a ceremony, which involved the handing over of a staff, spear, sword, or other symbol.[67]

Such an investiture ceremony came to be utilized for spiritual offices as well (especially in German territory), which caused great consternation to the ecclesial reformers of the eleventh century, who desired a Church free from any form of secular control and interference. Their desire to eradicate the practice of investiture resulted in a great controversy between pope and king. The crisis originated due to the structure of medieval society and the customs and traditions of the age but involved a greater question: whether it was the pope or the king who appoints bishops. The "investiture controversy" consumed the pontificate of one saintly bishop of Rome and negatively impacted the Church for nearly half a century.

Crisis

When Hildebrand left Rome in exile with the disgraced Pope Gregory VI (r. 1045–1046), who abdicated due to the crime of simony, he probably assumed he might never see his beloved city again. But when Bruno of Alsace became Pope Leo IX, he asked Hildebrand to return to the Eternal City to assist in his plan of reform for the Church. The spirited monk served as an adviser to the next five popes, living one of the most accomplished and influential lives of the eleventh century. Hildebrand was small of stature and not a handsome man, but his dogged determination, outstanding intellect, iron will, and personal sanctity made him a fierce opponent in any dispute. As a cardinal adviser to Pope Nicholas II, he championed the reform initiative whereby the cardinals

elected the pope, thus limiting the role of secular authority in papal elections. Although contented to remain behind
the scenes, Hildebrand was thrust into the limelight when
elected pope upon the death of Alexander II (r. 1061–1073).

Only a deacon at his election, Hildebrand was ordained
priest and then bishop and crowned pope over the span of a
month. He was fifty-three years old and the first pope from
Rome in nearly thirty years. Taking the name Gregory VII
(r. 1073–1085), he embarked on a papal agenda concentrated
on continuing and expanding the reform initiatives of his
predecessors. In his first year, Pope Gregory held a reform
council in Rome that issued four decrees aimed at eradicating the evils of simony and clerical sexual immorality.
Although previous pontiffs had issued similar decrees, Gregory added a new dimension by forbidding the faithful from
attending any services administered by clerics in violation
of the decrees. He sent papal legates throughout Christendom to inform and warn bishops, priests, and the laity about
his reform decrees. He expected obedience of clerics and
demanded secular authorities heed papal teaching.

Although previous popes had asserted primacy and universal jurisdiction in the Church and highlighted the supe-
riority of the spiritual power over the secular, Gregory
added a new element to the concept of the "two powers."
First formulated in the fifth century by Pope St. Gelasius
I (r. 492–496) in a letter to the Eastern emperor Anasta-
sius I (r. 491–518), the policy viewed the world according
to two powers: priestly and royal. Gelasius argued that the

spiritual authority of priests carried more weight than secular power because priests "have to render an account for even the kings of men in the divine judgment."[68] Although the early Church (notably St. Ambrose of Milan) believed the Christian emperor was not above rebuke from the Church in certain matters, Gelasius's teaching offered a distinction that placed ecclesial power on a superior plane. The view created tension (mostly healthy) in the West between the Church and the civil political power—unlike the situation in the East where the Church was subservient to the state, as emperors exercised the policy of *caesaro-papism*, which amounted to the state controlling the Church. Gregory's addition to the "two powers" formula consisted of viewing the priestly authority, especially the pope, as a moral *judge* and not just a moral teacher of kings and emperors. He agreed with the writings of the late Cardinal Humbert of Silva-Candida in his treatise *Against the Simoniacs* that ecclesial authority was superior to secular power:

> The priesthood of the Church is like the soul, the kingdom like the body; they have need of one another. But just as the soul dominates and commands the body, so is the priestly dignity superior to the royal dignity as heaven is to the earth. The priesthood must determine what is to be done . . . kings must follow the churchmen.[69]

Gregory believed that the pope could condemn kings and emperors and impose either private or public penances on them. The ultimate sentence of excommunication, according to Gregory, involved not only personal but public ramifications. An excommunicated king's soul was in grave danger and in need of reconciliation. Additionally, the sentence of excommunication freed a king's subjects from their oaths of fealty to him and opened the path to rebellion and deposition.

Gregory's vision of papal power was recorded in the papal register in 1075 as a list of twenty-seven decrees, known as the *Dictatus Papae*. These decrees illustrated clearly that Gregory was convinced of his superior authority in relation to secular rulers and provided the framework for the implementation of his reform policies. Among the decrees in the *Dictatus Papae* were the teachings that the pope alone can depose bishops; that the pope is the only man to whom all princes have to show obedience; that the pope can depose emperors; that ecumenical councils cannot be convened without papal approval; that the pope cannot be judged by anyone; that papal sentences cannot be repealed, and that the pope alone can repeal all other sentences.[70] Armed with his vision of papal authority, Gregory turned his attention to the next task in the papal reform movement: ridding the Church of secular interference in ecclesial appointments.

The method of choosing candidates for episcopal office has developed and changed over the course of the Church's history. In the early Church, bishops were elected by the clergy and people of a diocese but did not assume episcopal duties until consecrated by other bishops. After the collapse of Western Roman imperial government in the late fifth century, secular rulers began appointing bishops.[71] Beginning in the ninth century, secular rulers appointed bishops while the clergy and people of the diocese acclaimed the choice. In German territory, the right of the king to select bishops became a normal aspect of royal functions.

Secular rulers wanted control over episcopal appointments because bishops were reliable administrators and the office, along with its temporal land holdings, was not hereditary. As a result, in conflicts, the bishops of the realm tended to side with the king. In the ceremony appointing the bishop to his office, the secular lord gave secular symbols (a sword or spear) and spiritual symbols (ring and crozier) while saying "receive this church."[72] The new bishop took an oath of fealty to the king, performed an act of homage, and was then ordained, usually by the metropolitan bishop. This ceremony, although similar to the investiture of vassals, did not indicate that the ecclesiastical office was a fief but rather that the bishop was under royal protection and owed secular service to the king.[73] Regardless, the action gave the perception that the king's appointment made the bishop a vassal and that the diocese was the king's gift to him. Unsurprisingly, royal selection of bishops did not always result in the most spiritually suitable candidates—as witnessed by the sentiment of Archbishop Manassas of Reims who said, "The archbishopric would be a fine thing, if only one did not have to sing Mass for it."[74] Unsuitable candidates for the episcopacy caused all kinds of problems for the Church and led to continued corruption, scandal, and even heresy.

Although in 1059 Pope Nicholas II issued a papal ban against secular investiture of bishops, the practice continued. King of the Germans Henry IV (r. 1054–1105) staunchly defended his royal prerogative of episcopal appointments. Henry desired the title and crown of Holy Roman Emperor, which his father and grandfather had held, but the title required papal coronation. Henry IV was a powerful and stubborn man and his reign as king (and eventually as emperor) was marked by near-constant strife with the Roman pontiffs, as he was excommunicated five times by three different popes. His epic clash with Pope Gregory VII, which spawned one of the most prominent crises in Church history, began over the appointment of the archbishop of Milan.

The city was the site of an intense ecclesial reform movement in the mid-eleventh century. A group of cloth weavers, known as the *Patarenes* or "ragged ones" and led by Ariald of Varese and Landulf Cotta, called for an end to clerical abuses, especially simony. Violence erupted in the city, prompting Pope Nicholas II to send Peter Damian and Anselm of Lucca (the future Pope Alexander II) to negotiate a peace. Eventually, the citizens asked King Henry to intervene, and he began appointing bishops in the region.

When the archdiocese of Milan became vacant, Gregory and Henry disagreed on the choice of candidates. The king refused to relinquish his "right" of appointment, which provoked Pope Gregory VII to issue a decree in 1075 banning secular investiture and additional bans in 1078 and 1080. Henry viewed the pope's edicts as threats to his secular authority and impediments to his ability to govern the kingdom effectively. Supporters of the king, such as Benzo of Alba in his work *Ad Heinricum*, criticized the pope and insisted that bishops obey royal rather than papal authority: "[Bishops] were planted in the house of the Lord by the hands of the king . . . [they] cannot serve two lords [and] must be subject therefore to their planter, not to their supplanter [Hildebrand]."[75]

Pope Gregory VII knew that his decree would anger the king, so he sent ambassadors to Henry to dissuade him from further action. The papal envoys informed the king that any retaliatory behavior on his part would result in excommunication, which only served to raise the king's ire. Gregory's policies elicited harsh reactions from others as well. The pope was attacked by armed men under the command of the Roman nobleman Cencius Stephani on Christmas Eve 1075 while celebrating Mass in the basilica of St. Mary Major. Although there was no direct evidence of Henry IV's involvement in the attack on the pope, the event heightened Gregory's awareness of danger from secular rulers.

Upset at the message delivered by the papal ambassadors, King Henry IV summoned an emergency meeting of the *Diet*, a consultative body composed of German nobility and clerics, at the city of Worms. There he unleashed a diatribe of spiteful language about the pope and subsequently sent a letter to Rome in which he condemned Gregory as a perjurer, adulterer, illegitimately elected, and a menace to the peace of Christendom, writing, "By the sword you have come to the throne of peace and from the throne of peace you have destroyed the peace."[76] The king's anger was even conveyed in the letter's salutation, which began, "To Hildebrand, at present not pope but false monk."[77] Henry accused Pope Gregory of simony and urged him vehemently to resign the papacy: "Let another ascend the throne of St. Peter, who shall not practice violence under the cloak of religion, but shall teach the sound doctrine of St. Peter. I Henry, king by the grace of God, do say unto thee, together with all our bishops: Descend, descend, to be damned throughout the ages."[78] Shocked at the contents of the king's letter and following through on the promise delivered by his ambassadors, Pope Gregory VII excommunicated Henry IV in February 1076 and absolved royal subjects from their oaths of fealty:

> I take from King Henry, son of the Emperor Henry, who has risen against the Church with unheard-of pride, the government of the entire kingdom of the Germans and of the Italians. And I absolve the Christian people from any oath that they have taken, or shall take, to him. And I forbid anyone to serve him as king.[79]

Gregory's unprecedented action established a new level of tumult in the relationship between Church and state. Henry was viewed in ecclesial reform circles as a persecutor of the Church akin to the Roman emperors of old, as Heribert, bishop of Reggio, wrote, "What was Nero, what was Diocletian, what final[ly] is [Henry] who at this time persecutes the Church: surely they are all the gates of hell?"[80] Pope Gregory hoped the German nobility would rise and recognize a new king, which did occur in 1077, but before that happened the wily Henry embarked on an utterly startling course of action that placed the pope in a precarious situation.

Following the king's excommunication, the German nobles assembled and ordered Henry to reconcile with the pope within four months or be deposed. The nobles also requested Pope Gregory's presence at the next Diet planned at Augsburg in 1077. Gregory left Rome on his way to German lands but stopped at Canossa in northern Italy to spend the winter, since traveling over the Alps at that time of year was treacherous. The castle at Canossa was in the territory of papal ally Countess Matilda of Tuscany (1046–1115), a fierce warrior, political leader, and influential secular ruler.[81] Receiving news that the pope was wintering over in Canossa, Henry and a small entourage decided to cross the Alps during the severe winter weather in order to seek the pope's forgiveness. The journey was so dangerous that members of Henry's traveling party lost limbs due to frostbite. Finally, an astonished Gregory learned that Henry was outside the castle begging for an audience.

The penitential king remained outside for three days as the pope contemplated how to respond to this unique situation. It is possible that the pope allowed the king to remain outside the castle for days in order to teach him a lesson, but it is also possible that Gregory was undecided on the right course of action. If he readily admitted the king and granted the requested absolution, the German nobility who had summoned the pope to the Diet would feel betrayed; however, the refusal of mercy to a contrite penitent would be a betrayal of the pope's priestly responsibilities. Gregory finally allowed the king entrance, and the two men reconciled their differences with one important distinction: the pope forgave the king's impetuousness and lifted the excommunication but did not restore Henry to the throne, since that question remained an agenda item on the upcoming Diet. In a later letter, Gregory made certain that his decision at Canossa was understood properly:

I restored him to communion only, but did not reinstate him in the royal power from which I had deposed him in a Roman synod. Nor did I order that the allegiance of all who had taken oath to him or should do so in the future, from which I had released them all at that same synod, should be renewed.[82]

The king promised to obey Gregory's future commands, safe passage to German territory to meet the nobles, and to abide by papal and noble judgment on whether he should retain the royal title.[83] Henry's confession at Canossa assuaged most of his former noble supporters, who rallied to his cause. A group of rebels, though, declared Henry deposed and in the spring of 1077 elected Rudolf of Swabia, Henry's brother-in-law, king. Gregory VII was torn between the two candidates and took three years to make a definitive judgment: in favor of Rudolf.

Despite his promises and ostentatious show of piety at Canossa, Henry reverted to his old habits of lay investiture and disobedience to the pope, prompting another excommunication and deposition from Gregory in the spring of 1080. A few months later at the council of Brixen, Henry declared Gregory deposed as pope and appointed as (anti) pope Wibert, archbishop of Ravenna, who took the name Clement III. Henry and his army defeated Rudolf and the rebels in German territory and then marched to Rome, where they besieged the city for three years. Eventually, Henry's troops breeched the defensive walls and poured into the city. Pope Gregory VII fled to the fortress of Castel Sant'Angelo for refuge. Once in the city, Henry's antipope Clement III crowned the king emperor. Gregory sent word requesting the military aid of the Normans in southern Italy, who marched on Rome, prompting Henry to return to his imperial territory. When the Normans arrived at Rome (with a large contingent of Muslim troops), they sacked the city for three days, destroying a third of the city by fire.[84] Blamed for the rampage, Gregory VII fled Rome and died in exile on May 25, 1085.

Pope St. Gregory VII centered his pontificate on the task of reforming the Church and freeing it from the interference of secular rulers. Near the end of his life, the valiant pope wrote a letter expressing his ardent concern for the Church and that it "should return to her own proper dignity and remain free, chaste and catholic. But because these things were greatly displeasing to the ancient enemy, he armed his members against us to defeat them."[85] Nearly forty years after his death the "Investiture Controversy" ended in part thanks to Gregory's staunch defense of ecclesial authority and jurisdiction. Pope Callistus II (r. 1119–1124) and King Henry V (r. 1099–1125) agreed that investiture of ecclesial and secular symbols should be separated and conferred by members of the respective spheres (spiritual symbols from clerics and secular symbols from lords). The compromise was initially agreed to in the Concordat of Worms in 1122 and later ratified at the First Lateran Council in 1123.

Renewal

Although the struggle between Church and state was far from over, the crisis of investiture and Pope St. Gregory VII's defense of ecclesial independence laid the foundation for a renewed, invigorated, and powerful papacy in the later medieval period and, moreover, made a powerful statement to secular rulers that the Church would not be their puppet.

The papal reform momentum continued in the late eleventh century with the pontificate of Bl. Urban II (r. 1088–1099), who initiated the Crusading movement at the Council of Clermont in 1095. The Crusades exemplified the central role of the papacy in medieval Christendom as warriors responded in large numbers to the pope's urging to participate in those armed pilgrimages to the Holy Land and North Africa. Although a healthy tension still existed between the Church and temporal powers, the Crusades provided an avenue for ecclesial and secular cooperation. Secular rulers did not merely obey papal commands—indeed, papal letters directing courses of action were often ignored by Crusaders—but there was a general sense of collaboration, especially at the beginning of a campaign. Utilizing the earlier foundation provided by Popes Leo IX, Gregory VII, and Urban II, the papacy in the early thirteenth century reached the zenith of power, authority, and influence in Church history. This reinvigorated papacy shaped medieval society, provided central leadership, and swung the pendulum of spiritual-secular relations solidly in the direction of the Church.

Lothar of Segni came from a noble Roman family. His uncle reigned as Pope Clement III (r. 1187–1191) and created the young man a cardinal. Lothar was a brilliant student who began his education studying theology and law in Rome and completed it in Paris and Bologna. As a student, he traveled to England and visited the shrine of St. Thomas Becket, the archbishop of Canterbury who had been murdered for defending the prerogatives of the Church from the royal interference of Henry II, king of England. A few years after his uncle's death, Lothar was elected pope early in the year 1198—the first pope with a university education. His election continued the long line of Italian popes in the twelfth century (there were only two non-Italian popes) and gave the Church its youngest pope, at thirty-seven, in a century and a half. A deacon when elected, Lothar received priestly and episcopal ordination and was crowned pope on the feast of the Chair of St. Peter (February 22, 1198). Lothar took the name Innocent III (r. 1198–1216) and proceeded on the longest papal reign of the thirteenth century. His papacy marked the transition from the "monk-popes" of the eleventh century to the "lawyer-popes" of succeeding centuries.[86]

Innocent III's perception and application of papal power drew strength from the actions of his eleventh-century predecessors. The assertion of papal power in Christendom was the main objective of his pontificate as illustrated by his favorite biblical passage: "See, I have set you this day over nations, and over kingdoms, to pluck up and to break down, to destroy and to overthrow, to build, and to plant" (Jer. 1:10). Innocent projected papal power through politics, ecclesial policy, reform initiatives, legislation, and the Crusading movement. He was the first pope to systematically use the title *Vicar of Christ* and greatly magnified the papacy's unique role and authority in Christendom.

Innocent clearly articulated his pontifical vision in his first papal address, which was a substantial statement on the relationship between spiritual and temporal power. Innocent defined the pope as someone "higher than man but lower than God."[87] Furthering the concept of the "two powers," Innocent advocated the supremacy of the spiritual power in the world but recognized the role and jurisdiction, within its own realm, of temporal power. Innocent believed that kings should assist the papacy in the work of extending the Faith and maintaining a just and Christian society. He advocated the idea that temporal power is *derived from* spiritual power; hence its inferiority. Early in his pontificate, he articulated this belief in a letter utilizing celestial objects to illustrate his point: "Just as the moon derives its light from the sun . . . so, too, the royal power derives the splendor of its dignity from the pontifical authority."[88]

Although asserting that the pope held absolute power, Innocent maintained that he should only intervene in temporal matters (outside of papal territory) on critical occasions, occupying the role of mediator and moral judge. In Innocent's mind, kings were superior in their own realms, but those territories were geographically confined. Papal power, on the other hand, extended throughout the entire world because the Roman pontiff was the earthly representative of Christ.

Pope Innocent III's vision of papal authority was illustrated in his dealings with King John of England (r. 1199–1216). Innocent placed England under interdict and excommunicated John because the king refused to accept the papal candidate, Stephen Langton, for the vacant archbishopric of Canterbury. John forbade Langton from even entering the country. The tenuous situation continued for years until Innocent finally declared John deposed and supported a threatened French invasion of England. The stubborn king finally acquiesced to the pope and agreed to recognize Langton as archbishop, allowed exiled English clerical supporters of the pope to return home, and, on his own initiative, made England a papal fief with annual feudal dues payable to Rome. Innocent then lifted the excommunication and interdict and defended John against the rebellious nobles who compelled the king to sign the Magna Carta document. The pope declared the Magna Carta null and void not because of its content but rather its creation: England was a papal fief and the obligations imposed on the king by the nobles in the document were made without the pope's consent.

Pope Innocent III continued the reform efforts of his predecessors and sustained the campaign against simony, clerical sexual immorality, and eradicating secular interference in Church affairs. He recognized that the permanence of the reform initiatives rested on a reorganization of the papal curia and a renewal of the Church's episcopacy. The first phase of Innocent's reform efforts focused on papal bureaucracy, which he organized into three divisions: the Chapel, Chancery, and Chamber. The Chapel managed papal liturgical and ceremonial activities. The Chancery produced official papal correspondence and documents, including bulls (so called from the *bulla* or lead seals affixed to documents), and the Chamber controlled papal finances. Like his predecessors, Innocent recognized that ecclesial renewal efforts could not be merely dictated from Rome but needed to be enacted and enforced locally, which required the appointment of reform-minded and holy men as bishops and abbots. For these important ecclesial posts, he refused to appoint men who were easily influenced by secular pressure or temptation. Additionally, Innocent was not shy about removing prelates with divided loyalties and loose morals.

In an effort to limit the secular power exercised by bishops beholden to kings and lords, Innocent relied on papal legates (his own personal representatives in realms) and encouraged legal appeals to Rome. Innocent believed that a bishop's focus should be pastoral rather than princely and mandated that bishops perform pastoral visitations within their diocese as well as make *ad limina* ("to the threshold") trips to Rome every four years to report on the status of their diocese.

Innocent devoted great attention and energy to the Crusading movement, calling more Crusades than any other pontiff. The Crusading movement was a century old by the time of Innocent's reign and he instituted several innovations that furthered the concept, privileges, and administration of these armed pilgrimages. Crusading, for Innocent, was not merely a voluntary undertaking—it was a moral imperative. In *Quia Maior*, a 1213 bull, Innocent wrote, "To those men who refuse to take part . . . we firmly state on behalf of the apostle Peter that they . . . will have to answer to us on this matter in the presence of the Dreadful Judge on the Last Day of Severe Judgment."[89]

In order to encourage greater involvement, Innocent enlarged the spiritual benefits granted to Crusaders. He offered a plenary indulgence not only to those who fought in person but also to those who paid for a proxy to fight in their place, for the proxies themselves, and for those who provided material support to Crusaders. Although previous Crusades had been preached and approved by popes and clerics had participated in them, the management of these endeavors had been placed in the hands of secular lords. Innocent envisioned a greater oversight role of the papacy concerning the direction, management, and conduct of the Crusades. After the fiasco of the Fourth Crusade and its sack of Constantinople in 1204, Innocent appointed cardinals with command authority for the Fifth Crusade, which, sadly, still ended in disaster. Ensuring that a consistent message and objective was preached, Innocent appointed Crusade preachers under the direction of papal legates in every diocese of Christendom. Finally, in order to help finance the costly missions, Innocent III taxed the clergy and instituted the placement of "Crusade boxes" at the back of parishes for the faithful to deposit money. Despite these innovations, the Crusades called by Innocent III did not achieve their objective of liberating Jerusalem from Muslim occupation, but his improvements greatly shaped the future of the Crusading movement as future campaigns adopted his spiritual and temporal innovations.

The Fourth Lateran Council in 1215 was the penultimate achievement of Innocent's pontificate. Called by Innocent in his bull *Vineam Domini* in April 1213, this twelfth ecumenical council met to discuss plans for a new Crusade and to enact reform decrees for the renewal of the Church. Several thousand clerics attended the proceedings, and other important personages, including the religious reformers Francis and Dominic, were present in Rome during the conciliar meetings. The council addressed a growing heretical movement in southern France by stressing the importance of evangelization and catechesis, forbidding preaching without episcopal approval, and establishing a "master of theology" in every diocese to teach candidates to the priesthood.[90] The council also instituted the "Easter Duty" requiring all Catholics to confess their sins and receive the Eucharist at least once a year, preferably during the Easter season.

Sadly, Innocent did not live long enough to witness the impact of the Fourth Lateran Council on the Church or that of his reform and Crusading initiatives, as he died in July 1216. But the effects of Pope Innocent III's contribution to the papacy and its relationship with secular rulers lasted centuries and placed the Church in a position of influence and authority in medieval European society. Maligned by modern historians as a power-hungry absolutist monarch bent on world domination, Innocent was in fact rather a holy man focused on ensuring the continuance of the Faith and the security of the Church. The light of his accomplishments would not have been possible without the struggles and sacrifices of his papal predecessors who endured—and fought—the darkness of secular encroachment on ecclesial independence.

Although blessed at times with secular rulers committed to the spread of the Gospel and unity with the Church (such as the saintly Louis IX of France), the Church would continue to suffer at the hands of selfish secular lords desirous of controlling Christ's bride. The popes of the eleventh through the thirteenth centuries worked tirelessly to ensure the Church's independence by a commitment to internal reform and renewal. Their efforts produced the time of the "Glory of Christendom" and a golden age in Church history.[91]

5

The Albigensian Heresy

Christendom saw in heresy the specter of its own destruction; for to embrace heresy is to mutilate the figure of Christ, to parody the Church's teaching, to misunderstand the authority of God present in his Church, to inflict a mortal wound upon society, and to imperil the whole Christian world.[92]

—Henri Daniel-Rops

THE DARKNESS:
A gnostic heresy in southern France was infecting the Church with radical and destructive false teachings that ignorant and worldly clergy were impotent in combating.

THE LIGHT:
Systematic legal and spiritual measures emerged to eradicate religious error and reconcile repentant heretics, while revolutionary new religious orders focused on preaching sound doctrine, embracing holy poverty, and living virtuously.

Background

While the early Church was suffering violence from the Roman Empire, heresy was also infecting it from within. Church Fathers devoted considerable time and effort challenging and eradicating false teachings that threatened the unity of the Church and the eternal souls of the faithful. After legal recognition of the Faith in the early fourth century by the emperor Constantine ended the persecutions, the origination and orientation of heresy also changed. As more Roman citizens became Christian, they also questioned the Church's teachings concerning Christ. How can God be man? What is Jesus' relationship to the Father and to the Holy Spirit? The Christological controversies thus dominated the Church's attention from the fourth to the eighth centuries.

However, these heresies erupted in the eastern half of the Church and, with the exception of Arianism, which infested the western Germanic tribes, remained eastern issues. After the collapse of the western Roman Empire in the late fifth century, the Church in the West rarely dealt with heretical movements. Disruptions dominated the political and social landscape but unity in faith became the bedrock of

Christendom. So when attacks against the Church's teachings returned in the West and heretical movements attracted followers, Christians viewed these as an active threat to the political and social order. Heresy was not simply a matter of opinion but an attack on the foundations of ecclesial and secular authority and thus social unity.

In the Middle Ages, European society was imbued with Catholicism, its teachings, and its sacraments. The Faith was a unifying force that transcended political structures. Medieval people were theocentric in their worldview and oriented toward eternity. Earthly life was considered a pilgrimage and a transitional stage on the way to communion with God and the saints. Additionally, medieval society was hierarchical, which by its nature is unequal and authoritative. Medieval people accepted the class stratification in their society and its authoritative nature, which was imposed through violent means at times but mostly through societal norms.[93] In this milieu, heresy could not be tolerated because it attacked the social, political, and ecclesial order, often resulting in violence.

Not just the Church, therefore, but secular rulers thus viewed heresy as an active threat to their authority and were concerned with the instability and violence it produced in their realm. Accordingly, the secular arm punished heresy severely, usually with the death sentence. And the Church focused on preserving the faithful from the contagion of false teachings that placed souls in eternal danger. It was the duty of everyone in medieval society to combat heresy and its spread, and failure to do so, especially by secular rulers, was as bad as embracing the heresy itself. Yet secular rulers faced difficulty in combatting heresy since they and their agents were not trained theologians and did not understand the nuances of heretical beliefs.

However, a legal development occurred in the twelfth century that provided the Church and secular rulers with the structure and procedures necessary to eradicate heresy.

The adoption of imperial Roman legal procedure by the Church was perhaps the most significant intellectual and institutional development in medieval society.[94] Influenced by Roman law, the Church began the formation of a universal canon law. Although attempts at developing an ecclesial legal framework had occurred previously, the first universal canon law collection was accomplished in the twelfth century by the theologian and lawyer Gratian. His *Decretum* was a systematic compilation of the writings of Church Fathers, conciliar decrees, and papal writings. In the following century, the Dominican St. Raymond of Peñafort (1175–1275) wrote the *Liber Extra*, which added to Gratian's work and solidified canon law until the twentieth-century revision by Pope St. Pius X. The compilation, systematization, and codification of canon law resulted in a change in legal procedure that replaced accusatorial process with the inquisitorial process.

Prior to the twelfth century, legal procedure in medieval society was rooted in *accusatorial* procedure. Secular and ecclesial authority did not investigate crimes but rather victims, or their family, approached the institutions of authority and demanded satisfaction. The accuser went to court, made an accusation, swore an oath to its truthfulness, and called the other party to court to answer the charge. The accused appeared before the competent authority and swore an oath that the accusation was false (or admitted fault).[95] Doubt concerning the veracity of the accused's oath could result in undergoing an ordeal or judicial combat. Belief in the manifestation of God's judgment concerning innocence and guilt led to the practice of ordeals whereby the accused would undertake a dangerous feat, such as thrusting a hand into boiling water or picking up a hot iron. Lack of physical harm or healing of injury after a period of time proved the accused's innocence—or guilt if injury occurred or healing did not.

The implementation of *inquisitorial* procedure revolutionized the prosecution of criminal activity. Rather than relying on the initial accusation of crimes, the competent authority took an active role in investigating possible criminal activity. The process required the collection of evidence and testimony, either from witnesses or confession from the accused. The inquisitorial approach resulted in either a guilty or innocent judgment from the secular or ecclesial authority. Medieval society contained multiple legal courts with specific jurisdiction over offenses. Manorial courts dealt with civil disputes between peasants. Royal or local secular courts dealt with capital crimes committed by non-clerics. And Church courts existed to punish offenses against the moral law, crimes committed by clerics, and, beginning in the late eleventh century, heresy.

The eruption of a violent and pervasive heresy in southern France in the thirteenth century occasioned a major crisis for the Church and medieval society. The legal revolution allowed the prosecution of heresy and its concomitant eradication, aiding a revolution in religious life that spawned a renewal in faith.

Crisis

In the early eleventh century, a movement appeared in southern France that had migrated from the East and was reminiscent of the Gnostics—a heretical group from the Church's early history that believed in the goodness of spiritual things and the evil of material things. St. Irenaeus of Lyons (140–202) combatted the falsehoods of the Gnostics, as did St. Augustine (354–430) later in the fourth century when the heresy transformed into Manicheanism. The Church dealt initially with the resurgence of these heretical teachings through local councils at Toulouse (1119) and Tours (1163), and the great St. Bernard of Clairvaux (1090–1153) preached against the false beliefs in the mid-twelfth century. Despite the preaching and conciliar condemnations, the heresy spread rapidly, especially in the region of Albi, whence the heresy derived one of its names, *Albigensianism*. The dangerous heresy was also known as *Catharism* from the Greek *katharos* meaning "clean or pure."

Languedoc, the region in southern France infected with the hazardous heresy, was unique in the medieval period. It was not royal territory, and the French monarch exercised very limited control over it. The people spoke a different language from northern French; the dialect was closer to Castilian in neighboring Spain. Indeed, a merchant from the area could be easily understood in Barcelona but would need an interpreter in Paris![96] The region was more urbanized than northern France, and its towns, run by councils of citizens, were more powerful than the secular nobility. The most important town was Toulouse, whose secular ruler was politically weak, which contributed to the spread and success of the heresy.

The Church in the territory suffered from crooked, worldly, ignorant, illiterate, and unchaste clerics. Ecclesial abuses were prevalent with celibacy flouted, and simony, absenteeism, and pluralism were rampant. Priests could not rely upon bishops for proper leadership or direction, as they were the worst offenders—as evidenced by the stark rebuke of their behavior from Pope Innocent III:

> [The bishops are] blind men, dumb dogs who can no longer bark . . . men who will do anything for money. All of them, from the greatest to the least are zealous in avarice, lovers of gifts, seekers of rewards. Through such men the name of the Lord is blasphemed . . . They say the good is bad and the bad is good; they turn light into darkness and darkness into light, sweet to bitter and bitter to sweet. They do not fear God nor respect man . . . They give church offices to illiterate boys whose behavior is often

scandalous. The chief cause of all these evils is the arch-bishop of Narbonne, whose god is money, whose heart is in his treasury, who is concerned only with gold. This man, in his ten years as archbishop, has never visited his province or even his diocese.[97]

The poor example of Catholic clergy contributed to a general acceptance of indifference in the face of heresy, which was not the case in other areas of Christendom. In Languedoc, heretics and Catholics lived together peace-fully. Heretics numbered among the family members and friends of clerics, and families continued to associate with heretical relatives. The general feeling in the region was that accepting false teaching was not wrong and heresy was not a serious problem.[98] Embracing heresy in Languedoc resulted in no serious social or political ramifications. Indeed, her-etics were members of the city council in Toulouse. Secular authorities did not regard combatting heresy as necessary; Bishop Fulk of Toulouse asked the knight Pons Adhemar of Roudeille why he did not prosecute heretics in his lands, and the knight replied: "We cannot; we were brought up with them, there are many of our relatives among them, and we can see that their way of life is a virtuous one."[99]

Although the heretics in Languedoc may have lived seem-ingly virtuous lives and appeared non-threatening, their beliefs placed the souls of the faithful in grave danger and the organized structure of their movement endangered the Church and its authority in medieval society. The Cathars believed in a dualistic system of good and evil, wherein the world was the stage of conflict between the god of light (spiritual things) and the god of darkness (material things). In Cathar theology, Satan, the highest of angels, rebelled against God and created the material world, including the first man and woman. The first humans were only created from material elements and did not possess a soul. God took pity upon these creatures and gave them souls, but they rebelled and committed the original sin of engaging in the sexual act, which imprisoned a good spiritual soul in an evil material body. Cathars believed that the sexual act was the greatest sin, and strict believers were forbidden to marry. If they were tempted sexually, accommodations were made for homosexuality and bestiality since procreation could not result.[100]

Trapped in an evil material body, humanity required intervention from the spiritual world to escape the physical world. So, God sent Jesus to humanity. According to Cathar belief, Jesus was neither God nor man but rather a phantom that preached spiritual release so that the soul could be freed from the confines of the evil prison of the body. Jesus, as a spiritual entity, only appeared to suffer and die on the cross and was not truly present in the Eucharist. Jesus' original teachings, they claimed, were garbled by the Catholic Church but faithfully preserved in the Cathar church. Membership in that church provided access to Jesus' original secret teachings and helped humanity achieve freedom from the evil effects of the material world.

One of the most dangerous and disruptive Cathar beliefs was this claim that the Catholic Church distorted Jesus' original teachings. Its ancillary teaching that only the Cathar church was the true church was a dire threat to the peace and unity of Christendom. St. Dominic experienced this Cathar heresy while traveling through the region in 1207, hearing a heretic say, "The Roman church is the devil's church, and her doctrines are those of demons; she is the Babylon whom St. John called the mother of fornication and abomination, drunk with the blood of saints and martyrs . . . neither Christ nor the apostles established the existing order of the Mass."[101]

The Cathars mimicked the structure of the Catholic Church with an organized hierarchy, dioceses, and clergy. This anti-church was led by the *Perfect,* or the elite members of the group, both male and female, who renounced the world by refusing to marry and own property. They practiced extreme forms of penance and fasting and ate a pescatarian diet because animal flesh and any food (except fish) derived from animal sexual intercourse was evil. The Perfect were "ordained" in a solemn public ceremony known as the *consolamentum*, which required a yearlong preparation and was reminiscent of baptism and ordination. The ritual consisted of a general confession (the *servitium*), recitation of the Lord's Prayer, denial of the Catholic faith and Church, and taking a promise (the *melioramentum*) to the Cathar church.[102] Once "ordained," the Perfect were allowed to perform Cathari rituals and expected to remain sinless and free from any attachments to the material world. As they aged, the Perfect prepared to undergo the *endura*, or death by starvation or other forms of suicide, as the ultimate act of worship in order to free their good spiritual soul from the confines of the evil material body.

Most devotees of the heresy were known as "believers" who, unlike the Perfect, could eat meat, marry, and engage in sexual activity. They joined in a liturgy known as the "Transmission of the Lord's Prayer," in which a passage from the New Testament was read, a homily was given by a Perfect, the Our Father was recited, and a sacred meal was shared. In order to hide their heretical behavior, believers were allowed to continue to receive Catholic sacraments. The rejection of the goodness of matter led the Cathari to embrace an anti-Christian worldview that threatened the very fabric of society. If material things are evil, then Christ could not have become man, there was no need for the sacraments—which are visible *material* signs of invisible grace—and marriage and family life, the foundation of human relationships and society, were unnecessary and even destructive. Catharism was not simply a matter of a difference of opinion or the expression of personal religious freedom; it was a mortal threat to Christian civilization.

Undoubtedly helping to spread the heresy was the sharp contrast between the apparent virtuous living of the Perfect and the greed and depravity displayed by Catholic clergy in Languedoc. Ignorant and immoral priests lacked the knowledge and the integrity to defend the Faith in word or deed from the Cathari's attack. Despite local condemnations, the heresy infected the region, and its spread sounded the general alarm in Rome during the pontificate of Innocent III. He renewed missionary efforts to the region in hope that a concerted evangelization and catechetical campaign would stem the heretical tide. The pope also deposed incompetent and immoral bishops and sent the holy Cistercian monk, Bl. Pierre de Castelnau (d. 1208) on a mission to convert the heretics and motivate the nobility to combat the heresy. Unfortunately, his mission was unsuccessful due to the scheming of the major secular ruler in the region.

Count Raymond VI of Toulouse (1156–1222) was the great-grandson of the famous Raymond IV, one of the major leaders of the successful First Crusade (1096–1102). However, Raymond VI was nothing like his well-known relative. A skeptical, devious, carnal, and reckless man, Raymond was not alarmed by the dangerous heresy infesting his territory. Though not a Cathar, he was sympathetic to the cause since his wife was a member (and possibly a Perfect). Due to Raymond's failure to combat the heresy in his realm, Pierre de Castelnau excommunicated him in 1207 and placed his lands under interdict. Worried by the ecclesial punishments, Raymond decided to meet with de Castelnau in January 1208 to restore communion with the Church.

The meeting was not cordial, however, and it ended with Raymond intimidating the papal legate. The next morning, Pierre de Castlenau was murdered under mysterious circumstances. There was no direct proof that Raymond was responsible for de Castelnau's death, but it was widely believed that he was, at the least, indirectly accountable for the crime. Angered by de Castelnau's death and Raymond's refusal to fight the heresy rampaging his lands, Pope Innocent III absolved Raymond's subjects from their fealty and declared him a murderer and heretic:

> We, according to the holy canons, by which fidelity is not owed to him who is not faithful to God, free from their oaths, as of our apostolic authority, all those who have sworn him fidelity, cooperation or alliance, and, the chief lord's rights being reserved, we give license to all Catholics to proceed against his person, and even to occupy and hold his land.[103]

After the Church had conducted a patient, concerted campaign of peaceful initiatives against Catharism for more than a half-century, Innocent III realized that more forceful means were needed to eradicate it and those secular rulers who supported it. Acceptance of the status quo was no longer possible. The pope proclaimed a Crusade against the heretics and those who supported them.

The ensuing conflict, though necessary for the spiritual and material defense of Christendom, turned into a nasty twenty-year civil war that ultimately abolished the independence of the region and increased royal control. Pope Innocent III recognized that Crusading in Languedoc was unlike a campaign to the Holy Land, so, he introduced several innovations to the Crusading movement. Instead of an armed pilgrimage to Jerusalem, the Crusade was defined as a period of military service to eradicate secular support for heresy. Additionally, warriors pledged forty days of service to the Crusade, which was the customary annual amount of time of military service a vassal owed a lord.

Although the changes to the Crusading movement generated sufficient manpower to commence the campaign, they also resulted in unintentional delays due to the constant departure and arrival of troops. Simon de Montfort (1160–1218), an accomplished warrior and devoted son of the Church with previous Crusading experience, led the campaign through most of its stages. The Crusade achieved results in the first year of 1209 as a result of Simon's strategy to besiege and capture strategic towns in the region. A momentous victory occurred at the Battle of Muret on September 12, 1213, when Simon's outnumbered force, lifted by the prayers of St. Dominic, defeated the forces of King Peter II of Aragon (1178–1213), who had come to the aid of his brother-in-law Raymond VI. Victory at Muret established Simon's reign as count of Toulouse, but Simon proved a harsh ruler and soon rebellious forces gathered under the leadership of Raymond VII, son of the deposed Raymond VI. Rebellion erupted in 1216, and over the next several years, Raymond VII succeeded in recapturing much of the territory occupied by the Crusaders. The Crusade suffered a devastating loss when Simon was killed on June 25, 1218 at the siege of Toulouse by a stone from a mangonel (a type of trebuchet) that struck his head.

The final stage of the Crusade involved royal participation when King Louis VIII (r. 1223–1226), took the cross in 1226. Later that year, royal forces captured Avignon from the heretics, but Louis VIII died a few months later, leaving his twelve-year-old son, Louis IX, as king. The Crusade ended and peace was achieved in 1229, when Raymond VII performed a public act of penance, received absolution and reconciliation to the Church, and was recognized as the count of Toulouse. In return, Raymond agreed to pay the king and the Church a large war indemnity, offer rewards for the capture of heretics, and provide salaries for professors of theology and canon law, which led to the foundation of a university in Toulouse.

Renewal

The crisis of the Albigensian heresy disrupted the peace and unity of the Church and society, threatened many souls with dangerous falsehoods, and ultimately led to a brutal and bitter civil war in which the king of France gained power over a previously independent region. And that violence interrupted the heretical movement but did not eradicate it. It also took the legal revolution of the twelfth century and the development of non-violent means to deal with the danger of heresy. Faced with the crisis in Languedoc, the Church focused on new ways of safeguarding its teachings and the souls of the faithful. The poor example of Catholic clergy had also led to the spread of heresy, and so from that crisis new religious orders developed, which increased spiritual fervor in the thirteenth and subsequent centuries.

The Church's legal campaign against heresy began in 1184 when Pope Lucius III (r. 1181–1185) issued the bull *Ad abolendam*. The bull comprised a list of heretical teachings sent to the bishops of Christendom. Pope Lucius ordered the bishops to take an active role in determining the guilt of heretics; theologians using Roman legal procedures were to examine those accused. Fifteen years later, in the bull *Vergentis in senium*, Pope Innocent III declared heretics and secular rulers who protected them to be traitors to God. Embracing heresy was a punishable crime that included the confiscation of goods and property. In the mid-thirteenth century, the Church formally instituted the procedures for inquisitors when Pope Gregory IX (r. 1227–1241) promulgated *Ille humani generis*, a bull that established the appointment of clergy as inquisitors and charged them with preserving orthodox Catholic beliefs and teachings. It mandated that the inquisitor should be at least forty years old, trained in theology, and notable for virtuous living.[104]

The pope appointed as the first inquisitor one Conrad of Marburg, who operated in German territory. Twenty years later, Pope Innocent IV (r. 1243–1254) assigned inquisitors to operate in Italy and divided it into Franciscan and Dominican zones. Initially, papally appointed inquisitors were itinerate, operating in a given area or wherever heresy arose, but over time permanent institutional tribunals, known as "Inquisitions," were established in the major cities and towns of Christendom. These tribunals, the most famous of which was in Spain, operated for centuries and were not fully abolished, except for the Roman tribunal, until the eighteenth and nineteenth centuries.

The mission of the inquisitor was to protect the unity and security of the Church and society from the contagion of heresy. As a matter of charity, the inquisitor worked to save the endangered soul of the heretic and to reconcile the wayward to the Church. Inquisitors desired the repentance and conversion of heretics. Failure to achieve this goal led to remanding the heretic to secular authorities, who viewed heresy as a capital offense punishable by death. When the inquisitors arrived in an active area of heresy, they gathered the people and local clergy and preached the importance of orthodox belief and the need for repentance and salvation. The inquisitor's jurisdiction did not extend to unbelievers but involved Christians only, since heresy is a post-baptismal denial of doctrine.[105] After their preaching mission, the inquisitors instituted a "period of grace," usually forty days, during which individuals could self-incriminate. A voluntary confession resulted in a suitable penance and reconciliation to the Church. After that period, the inquisitors accepted accusations of heresy from others. An investigation commenced, evidence was collected, and witnesses called to provide testimony. The accused were provided a list of charges and allowed to call friendly witnesses and cross-examine hostile ones. Additionally, the accused provided to the inquisitors a list of enemies, whose testimony was not considered valid. The inquisitors utilized strict procedures during their investigation and sought the confession of the heretic and his reconciliation.

The inquisitor's task was difficult since heresy is essentially an intellectual, spiritual, and voluntary crime. Eliciting a valid confession could prove problematic from a cagey heretic, as described by the French Dominican Bernard Guidonis (usually shortened to Gui), a famous inquisitor who battled Albigensians, Waldensians, the False Apostles, and the *Fraticelli* for decades, and wrote a manual for inquisitors known as the *Practica*. In his book *The Waldensian Heretics,* Bernard admitted that "it is exceedingly difficult to interrogate and examine the Waldensians, and to get the truth about their errors from them, because of the deception and duplicity with which they answer questions."[106] Bernard highlighted the struggle against wily heretics in an exchange with an accused Waldensian:

When he is asked if he knows why he has been arrested, he answers very sweetly and with a smile, "My Lord, I should be glad to learn the reason from you." Asked about the faith which he holds and believes, he answers, "I believe everything that a good Christian ought to believe." Questioned as to whom he considers a good Christian, he replies, "He who believes as Holy Church teaches him to believe." When he is asked what he means by "holy Church," he answers, "My lord, that which you say and believe is the holy Church." If you say to him, "I believe that the holy Church is the Roman church, over which the lord pope rules; and under him, the prelates," he replies, "I believe it. Meaning that he believes that you believe it.[107]

In medieval society, torture to illicit a confession had been a routine aspect of legal procedures, but it was not authorized for use by papal inquisitors until 1252, twenty years after their establishment. The use of torture in ecclesial inquisitorial investigations was guarded by a number of protocols and protections for the defendant. The method of torture was applied always by the secular authorities, since clerics were forbidden by canon law to engage in such behavior. The use of torture was voluntary, and many inquisitors, including Bernard Gui, disliked it and believed it ineffective. Torture was only used to elicit a truthful confession and was not utilized as punishment for its own sake. A decision to use torture could be appealed by the accused, and exemptions existed for groups of people, including children, pregnant women, and the elderly.[108] Torture sessions were meticulously recorded, physicians were present at them, and they could not result in loss of limb or life. The accused were shown the instruments of torture before application in the hopes of a quick confession without their use. Confession under torture had to be repeated freely the following day for valid use in the legal proceedings.

Punishment for the confession of heresy reflected the orientation of the competent authority. The Church

desired the salvation of the heretic and focused on reconciliation. Seeking repentance and conversion, the Church
applied a penitential punishment to confessed heretics
that included fasting, giving alms, going on a pilgrimage
(including participation in a Crusade), and the wearing of
penitential clothing. Concerned with the preservation of
peace and unity in society, secular authority punished heresy severely. Although obstinate heretics were remanded
to the state and faced the death penalty for their dangerous
beliefs, the vast majority of cases resulted in penitential
ecclesial punishments.[109]

The establishment of papally appointed inquisitors to safeguard the Faith against the dangers of heresy led to the final
eradication of Catharism in southern France, achieving what
a bloody twenty-year civil war failed to do. The crisis of the
Albigensian heresy forced the Church to evaluate the prosecution of heresy and develop non-violent means to protect
and preserve Christian society and save souls from eternal
damnation. The procedures, developed in the thirteenth century for the eradication of heresy and the preservation of the
Faith, served the Church through the ages with the creation
of institutional tribunals throughout Christendom and continues into the modern world in the Roman curia. Although
most of the institutional tribunals charged with investigating heresy were abolished in the post-Enlightenment era,
one, the Holy Office of the Inquisition in Rome, remained.
Renamed the Congregation for the Doctrine of the Faith
after the reforms of the Second Vatican Council, the work

of safeguarding authentic Catholic teaching from error and guiding souls on the true path to salvation continues.

The heresy crisis of the thirteenth century also produced renewal in religious life; whereas the early medieval period had been the time of the monk, the later Middle Ages now produced the age of the friar.[110] Remember that the apparent holiness of the Cathars and the immorality and incompetence of Catholic clergy in southern France contributed to the growth of heresy in the region. This state of affairs was witnessed by a young man from Castile during his travels through the area in the early thirteenth century. Born into a noble and holy family in Castile, Dominic (1170–1221) had accompanied his bishop on a mission for King Alfonso IX: to secure marriage for his son, Prince Ferdinand. Although their journey to a foreign nobleman resulted in a bride for the prince, the young woman died on the return trip, so Dominic and his bishop traveled to Rome where they met Pope Innocent III. The pope sent the pair to Languedoc to assist in combatting the Cathar heresy.

Dominic judged that the effective way to eradicate the heresy involved a well-educated, spiritually formed, and eloquent orthodox clergy. The local clergy did not have the intellectual and homiletic skills, or the prayer life required to counteract the heretics. Moved by the situation in southern France and responding to the call of the Holy Spirit, Dominic founded the Order of Preachers in 1215. The mendicant group dedicated their lives to preaching, teaching, imitating Christ in poverty, and combatting heresy. Pope Honorius III

(r. 1216–1227) approved the new order in 1216 and gave the friars a universal preaching mission. Because of their formation, education, and holy living, Dominicans were appointed as inquisitors and worked to save souls and protect Christendom from the poison of heresy. Dominic worked tirelessly for his order and the good of the Church but was only given a half decade to do so before his death. Despite the brevity of time, Dominic built a lasting legacy and contributed greatly to the reform and renewal of the Church.

While Dominic battled heretics in southern France, another young man in Italy became aware of his special calling to embrace holy poverty and renew the Church. Giovanni Bernardone, called Francis by his father who frequently traveled to France for business, was a solider and worldly man in his youth, but a trip to Rome and a vision inside a dilapidated church changed his life radically. Renouncing his wealth and worldly attachments in a dramatic and public fashion in 1208, Francis's simple and holy living attracted others who desired personal sanctification. Francis formed his followers into the Order of Friars Minor and received permission from Pope Innocent III to preach. Francis focused his group on the works of preaching, begging, and service to the poor in a joy-filled appreciation for the goodness and gifts of God. The Franciscans embraced holy poverty not for its own sake but because total detachment to material things helped the Christian on the path of salvation by imitating Christ. The holy man from Assisi and his band of followers provided an authentic example of virtuous Christian living in the midst of temporally focused and spiritually inept secular clergy.

Although the charisms of the two new groups were different, they both pursued mendicancy (begging for sustenance), the first religious orders in Church history to do so. Both orders became agents of reform and renewal at a time of great wealth in the Church and were utilized by the papacy in the task of ecclesial transformation. The friars of Dominic and Francis changed the Church and the world through their revolution in a spiritual life focused on embracing simplicity and poverty. Sacrificing the cares of the world by complete abandonment to divine providence, the Franciscans and Dominicans were able to focus exclusively on their charisms of preaching, service to the poor, and combatting heresy. Their work renewed the Church in the medieval world and provided a constant reminder of authentic Christian living, especially in times of spiritual crisis.

6

Avignon and the Great Western Schism

If we turn to the prelates, they devote themselves so much to their own affairs and live so luxuriously, that they do not seem to care when they see their subjects in the hands of demons.[111]

—St. Catherine of Siena

THE DARKNESS:
A crisis in the papacy produced the abuse of absenteeism when seven popes spanning nearly seventy years lived in southern France rather than Rome. Their return to the Eternal City produced another calamity as anti-popes produced a schism lasting a generation.

THE LIGHT:
The papal crisis and poor state of the clergy led Catholic faithful to establish confraternities and associations in order to nourish their faith life. These groups did not rebel against the Church or its hierarchy but rather focused on reform of self in imitation of Christ.

Background

Perhaps no greater century of crisis afflicted the Catholic Church than the fourteenth. Later centuries would see the cleaving of Christendom resulting from disruption of the Protestant movement, the persecution of the Church, and deaths of millions of Christians, but the fourteenth century witnessed traumatic external and internal upheaval that altered the fabric of Christian society and caused long-term harm to the Bride of Christ.

The early years of the century beheld crop failures and a great famine that killed thousands in northern Europe. A decade later began the Hundred Years War, a deadly and destructive conflict between the kingdoms of England and France punctuated by occasional periods of peace. In the middle of the century, a great pestilence from the east arrived, infecting every country in Christendom except Poland and Bohemia. This "Black Death" plague devastated Catholic Europe, killing fifty percent of the entire population[112]—among the dead a high percentage of clergy who perished ministering to the sick and their families and burying the multitude of dead. Adding to the disruption of the age were several peasant rebellions in Flanders, France, and England.

For the Church, the end of the thirteenth century involved short pontifical reigns and long deliberations by the cardinals to elect papal successors. As an example, when Pope Clement IV (r. 1265–1268) died, it took nearly three years for the cardinals to elect Bl. Gregory X (r. 1271–1276). The interregnum would have lasted longer still had not the people of Viterbo, where the cardinals had gathered, locked the cardinals in the palace to force a decision. Even that measure lasted a year as the cardinals, mired in bickering, could not agree on a candidate. Finally, the people embarked on a more radical solution, removing the roof of the palace in order to expedite a decision, which occurred three days later!

Sadly, the political posturing and national rivalries among the cardinals did not improve in the fourteenth century, which produced popes focused on the temporal exercise of power. These popes made imprudent political decisions and used the spiritual weapons of interdict and excommunication for political purposes. Their policies created resentment for the papacy throughout Christendom. Papal taxes, for example, increased in order to service the large papal debt accumulated to finance various wars. Whereas previous centuries illustrated the papacy's role in initiating and implementing reform and renewal measures throughout the Church, the fourteenth-century papacy, in which only two popes (Bl. Benedict XI and Bl. Urban V) were recognized for sanctity, created a *need* for reform and renewal in the

Church.[113] The end result was a papacy in significant crisis with both its spiritual and political power in decline. This weakened Church unity and laid the foundation for the breaking-apart of Christendom in the sixteenth century.

The crisis in the fourteenth-century papacy began during the first pontificate of the century. Boniface VIII (r. 1294–1303), the nephew of Pope Alexander IV (r. 1254–1261) and a skilled lawyer, served as a papal diplomat for thirty years before his election as a successor of St. Peter. His papacy began with controversy as he arrested and imprisoned his predecessor, the saintly Celestine V (r. 1294).

Celestine's pontificate had begun with great promise but ended in abject failure. An eighty-four-year-old former hermit, the former Peter Murrone had come to the papacy through unique means. Concerned about the impact to the Church from a two-year papal interregnum, Murrone wrote a letter to Cardinal Latino Malabranca Orsini in the summer of 1294 urging the cardinals to elect a pope. The hermit was surprised to learn subsequently that the cardinals elected *him*. Murrone reluctantly accepted election, taking the name Celestine, and reigned as pope for only five months in Naples (he never set foot in Rome) before realizing that he lacked the skills to reign as supreme pontiff. So, Celestine abdicated, paving the way for the Italian cardinal Benedict Gaetani's election as Boniface VIII. The new pope embarked on an agenda of asserting ecclesial independence of secular control akin to previous papal reform programs, but Boniface's approach lacked charity and created unnecessary controversy.

Although Boniface angered multiple monarchs, it was his relationship with King Philip IV, "the Fair" (r. 1285–1314), that dominated his pontificate. Though he was personally pious, the grandson of King St. Louis IX did not embrace his saintly predecessor's relationship with the Church and papacy. Philip desired absolute control in France, which included control over the Church. Doggedly pursuing this royal agenda with him was William of Nogaret (c. 1260–1313), a lawyer, royal adviser, and progeny of heretical parents. Nogaret was a consummate minion, described by a contemporary as "a body without a soul, who cared nothing about anyone's rights but only wants to increase the wealth of the king of France."[114]

The conflict between pope and monarch centered on money. The Fourth Lateran Council in 1215 decreed that clergy could not pay taxes levied by secular rulers without papal consent.[115] However, this prohibition was ignored by the kings of England and France, who taxed the Church to pay for their wars. In an attempt to stop this royal abuse of power, in February 1296 Boniface VIII issued the bull *Clericis laicos*, which forbade clerics to pay taxes to secular lords and required papal approval of any royal tax on the Church. Failure to comply resulted in excommunication with absolution reserved to the pope.

Receipt of the bull in France was not positive. Philip felt threatened and issued his own policies—including withholding the export of money from France without royal approval. This measure blocked the flow of funds to Rome, triggering great papal concern. The relationship between king and pope continued to deteriorate into the new century, provoking a greater crisis: angered by Boniface's policies and behavior, Philip attacked the Church by arresting Bishop Bernard Saisset of Pamiers on trumped-up charges of blasphemy, heresy, and treason. After a secular trial the bishop was convicted and imprisoned and the king brazenly submitted the verdict to Rome for papal approval. Boniface rejected the shameless request and commanded that the bishop be immediately released.

Instead, the royal-papal relationship descended further into animosity when Boniface issued the bull *Ausculta fili* ("Listen, son!") in December 1301. The pope rebuked the king, exhorting him to "let no one persuade you that you have no superior or that you are not subject to the head of the ecclesiastical hierarchy, for he is a fool who thinks so."[116] Boniface threatened Philip with excommunication and remarked later that "if the king of France does not behave himself properly, I shall have the unpleasant duty to depose him like a little boy."[117] Wishing to rid the king of the quarrelsome pontiff, the royal sycophant Nogaret devised a plan to seize Boniface and force him to abdicate so that Philip could install his own pope. In September 1303, Nogaret assembled a military force to storm the papal palace in Anagni, Boniface's hometown, where the pope was staying. The raid succeeded in capturing Boniface, but word quickly spread that the pope was held hostage by a rogue force, and two days later the townspeople of Anagni attacked the palace and freed him. Nogaret escaped to France, but the audacious attack and physical toil impacted Boniface's health and he died a month later.

Finally free of the cantankerous pontiff, Philip meddled in Church affairs so that a favorable papal candidate was elected. That pope made a decision that set the Church on the path of crisis from which it suffered for more than a century.

Crisis

The brief reign of Bl. Benedict XI (r. 1303–1304), who died mysteriously one day before he was to excommunicate the toady Nogaret, marked the end of papal residence in Rome for the next seventy years. His successor Bertrand de Got, the archbishop of Bordeaux, was elected pope on June 5, 1305, taking the name Clement V. An esteemed canon lawyer and vassal of the French and English kings, de Got was a surprise papal candidate in that he was not a cardinal. He was not a strong leader, either, and Philip IV found he could easily encourage the new pope to pursue royal objectives. But although Pope Clement V agreed to various demands of the French king, he did not always pursue them zealously.

Philip wanted the French pope to conduct a trial concerning the actions of Boniface VIII, akin to the infamous ninth-century Synod of the Corpse but without an actual exhumation. Clement opened proceedings but dragged his feet in prosecution. Philip wanted the pope to suppress the Knights Templars because of their undue influence, power, and wealth in France. Although the military religious order was eventually suppressed at the Council of Vienne (1311–1312), Clement refused to pass judgment on their guilt over spurious charges brought by the king, and he distributed their land and wealth to other military orders. The one royal demand that Clement accepted was moving the papal residence to France. A few years into his pontificate, Clement V announced to the cardinals the relocation of the papacy to Avignon.

This small city of several thousand inhabitants in southeastern France was strategically located so that it took only five days for letters to reach Paris, eight days to Bruges, ten days to London, and less than two weeks to Venice and Rome.[118] Additionally, residence in the city protected the pope and curia from the constant infighting, violence, and influence of rival Italian noble families.[119] Although the news of Clement's relocation was shocking, it was not unusual for popes to live outside of Rome proper; indeed, popes spent only eighty-two of the 200 years from the twelfth to the beginning of the fourteenth century living in the Eternal City.[120] And, as a temporal ruler, the pope held numerous territory outside of Rome, including Avignon. Nonetheless, the move to southern France was seen by other secular rulers as influenced by the French king and the impact was a loss of respect for the papacy throughout Christendom.

Clement's decision ushered in the seventy-year "Avignon Papacy," during which, in essence, the papacy committed the ecclesiastical abuse of *absenteeism*—a bishop not residing in his diocese. The abuse was prevalent at the time and a source of much consternation. Sadly, with the bishop of Rome participating in such an abuse, the papacy was not morally able to enforce the residency requirement of other bishops.

The move to Avignon was intended as a temporary safeguard to escape the chaotic political and military environment of fourteenth-century Italy, but it turned into a chronic situation with long-term ramifications. During his nine-year pontificate, Clement V created all but one cardinal from France, so that when he died in 1314, the likelihood of another French pope was high and a return to Rome remote. And so Jacques Duèse, a former bishop of Avignon, replaced Clement V, taking the name John XXII (r. 1316–1334). This elderly man intended to return to Rome if the political conditions allowed but embarked on policies that made a return difficult. He reorganized the papal curia and, in the process, created a vast bureaucracy with little desire to live in Italy. Several thousand people lived and worked in the papal court, including those in the papal household, the cardinals, and the administrative and judicial departments of the curia. The vast papal machinery needed operating funds, which were partially provided by the implementation of *annates*, or the first year's revenue of a diocese from a newly installed prelate.

The next Avignon pope, Benedict XII (r. 1334–1342), reduced the number of clerics living in the city, focused on reform of religious orders (he was a Cistercian and continued to wear his habit after the papal election), funded the repair of St. Peter's in Rome, and desired a return to the city. Unfortunately, circumstances did not allow for a papal homecoming, so Benedict began a renovation of the bishop's residence in Avignon into a papal palace. After a quarter-century of refuge in Avignon, the temporary relocation appeared enduring as Clement VI (r. 1342–1352) made no attempt and voiced no intention to leave the city on the Rhône. However, a subsequent pope, the only one who lived in Avignon who was later recognized for sanctity, did the unthinkable and returned to Rome.

Bl. Urban V (r. 1362–1370) was neither a cardinal nor bishop when elected pope in the fall of 1362, but was the abbot of St. Victor's monastery in Marseilles—and before that a monk of Cluny. The newly elected pontiff with a reputation for holiness embarked on a path of ecclesial reform and fought against the abuses of simony and absenteeism. He resolved to return the papal residence to Rome and heeded the pleadings of St. Bridget of Sweden (1302–1373), who had begged numerous popes in Avignon to return home. The saintly pope left southern France in April 1367 and arrived in Rome to much fanfare in October. After sixty years of papal absence, the Eternal City was in shambles and the former papal palace at the Lateran was uninhabitable, so Urban V resided on Vatican hill.

The return to Rome was brief, as continued political infighting among the noble Roman families and a desire to negotiate an end to the Hundred Years War prompted Urban to leave the city despite the pleadings of the people and the saintly woman from Scandinavia. Urban left in the summer of 1370 and returned to Avignon but died before the year ended. Even the brief return of Urban V brought joy to the Church, especially in the Papal States, but his retreat to Avignon threatened prospects for a permanent homecoming and produced a despondent outlook on ending the "Babylonian Captivity" of the papacy.

It took a simple laywoman living as a Dominican tertiary in Siena to accomplish the seemingly impossible and convince Urban V's successor, Pope Gregory XI (r. 1371–1378) to return to Rome. Picking up the mantle of Bridget of Sweden, St. Catherine of Siena (1347–1380) sent letters to Gregory urging the pontiff to leave southern France. Catherine was well known in Christendom for her sanctity, spiritual writings, and extensive letters. She dictated her correspondence for years since she did not know how to write—a skill later given, miraculously, near the end of her life. Catherine developed a personal relationship with the pope and addressed him in letters as "daddy" and "our sweet Christ on earth." She could be also direct and fiery in her writings, harboring no patience for those who dallied in accepting and undertaking God's will. In the summer of 1376, Catherine decided to travel to Avignon to plead with Gregory in person. Accompanied by her confessor, Bl. Raymond of Capua (1330–1399), who acted as interpreter, Catherine met with Gregory and exhorted him to fulfill the vow he had made as cardinal. The revelation of his secret oath to God—that he would return the papacy to Rome if elected—by the humble young woman from Tuscany moved Gregory to accept her request.[121]

Her mission accomplished, Catherine returned to her beloved Siena.

Moving the papal court was no easy task; it required a large expense of funds at a time when the papal treasury was not full. French curial officials and cardinals were not thrilled with the idea of moving to Italy and even secular rulers believed that "Rome is wherever the pope happens to be."[122] In the face of opposition, Gregory delayed his departure (and received a stinging rebuke from Catherine[123]), but, eventually, the holy father left France and ended the papacy's long participation in the abuse of absenteeism.

The crisis of the Avignon Papacy was at an end, but its conclusion did not create peace and stability in the Church; instead, a new and graver danger erupted.

Pope Gregory XI died on March 27, 1378, and the subsequent conclave became one of the most controversial in Church history. Fearing that a long delay in electing a successor would result in a move back to France, Gregory stipulated that the conclave to elect his successor should not wait for any long-distance cardinals to arrive and that voting should be conducted by a simple majority.[124] Sixteen cardinals (eleven French, four Italian, and one Spaniard) gathered in Rome for the first conclave in the city in seventy-five years. Worried that the election of a French pope would move the papacy back to Avignon, the Roman people clamored for an Italian. Their desire was satisfied with the election of

Bartholomew Prignano, the archbishop of Bari (in southern Italy on the Adriatic coast), who took the name Urban VI (r. 1378–1389).

Urban was a well-known reformer and seemingly an excellent choice to succeed the beloved Gregory XI. However, Urban's temper, rudeness, and austere policies offended the cardinals. One prelate, angered by Urban's behavior, confronted the pope: "Holy father, you do not treat the cardinals with that honor which you owe to them, as your predecessors did; you are diminishing our honor, and I tell you in all truth that we shall do our best to diminish yours."[125] The threat became reality just five months after the papal election, when fifteen of the sixteen cardinals met to discuss the intolerable situation. Without ecclesial authority and ignoring their freely willed decision months early, these cardinals declared the election of Urban VI invalid due to the pressure and influence of the Roman people. They elected Cardinal Robert of Geneva as (anti-)pope, who took the name Clement VII. The result was the Great Western Schism, a crisis that affected Christendom for the next forty years.

Papal schisms were not new, indeed, the first schism had occurred in the third century and by the fourteenth century the Church had witnessed over thirty anti-popes. But the 1378 schism proved a calamity for the papacy and Christendom. Papal taxations and the seventy-year hiatus in Avignon had led to great resentment and loss of respect among secular rulers for the pope. Sentiment concerning the papacy and schism was illustrated by the writer and theologian Nicholas de Clémanges: "If the Roman church had not arrogated to itself the disposition over benefices of all ranks throughout the universal church, and had not despoiled all other churches, throttling their rights with its, this schism would never have occurred or, if it had occurred, would never have lasted so long."[126]

Secular rulers split their support between Pope Urban VI in Rome and the antipope Clement VII, who, after a failed attempt to conquer Rome by force, took up residence in Avignon. Urban VI excommunicated the rebellious cardinals and created new members of the college to replace them. Meanwhile, Clement VII created his own college of "anti-cardinals," further wracking the Church with division. An opportunity to end the schism presented itself when Clement VII died in 1394. Urban VI had died six years previously and was replaced by Boniface IX (r. 1389–1404), and the anti-cardinals of Clement VII could have ended the schism by supporting him, but they decided to elect as new antipope a member of the infamous anti-conclave of 1378: the Spaniard Pedro de Luna, who took the name Benedict XIII. Matters became more muddled in the early fifteenth century when cardinals from competing colleges gathered in Pisa and excommunicated and deposed the antipope Benedict XIII and Pope Gregory XII (who had replaced Innocent VII, the successor of Boniface IX), and elected a *new* antipope: Alexander V, who resided in Pisa. A low point in papal history was reached with three men claiming to be pope.

The papal schism created a constitutional crisis in the Church, as previous theological principles such as papal primacy and supremacy and the role and function of ecumenical councils were challenged. Heretics embraced old and new falsehoods about the Church, its constitution, and its hierarchy. The teachings of Marsilio of Padua (1275–1342), a scholar at the University of Paris, became popular. Marsilio advocated *conciliarism*: the belief that supreme ecclesial authority resided in the bishops gathered in an ecumenical council and not with the pope, who held instead a primacy of honor. The English Franciscan William of Ockham (1287–1347), who had spent time in the papal curia at Avignon, promoted conciliarism as well, and wrote a treatise titled *Eight Questions on the Power of the Pope.*

The Great Western Schism only came to an end through the actions of a secular ruler who needed a united Christendom in order to fend off the Ottoman Turks attacking his borders. Sigismund, king of the Germans and later holy Roman emperor, called an ecumenical council to meet at Constance (in modern-day Germany) to end the division. At the council, the anti-popes in Avignon and Pisa were deposed; Pope Gregory XII approved the convocation of the council and then abdicated the papacy in order to allow for the election of a candidate agreeable to all parties. Voting was conducted by nation and resulted in the election of Oddo Colonna, who took the name Martin V, in 1417. The advocates of conciliarism received support with the issuance of two decrees at Constance: *Sacrosancta* expressed the belief that all Christians, including the pope, must obey the decrees of ecumenical councils and *Frequens* stipulated the calling of the next council within five years of the end of Constance, the next council seven years after that, and then a council every decade.[127]

Pope Martin V (r. 1417–1431) was a committed reformer who worked tirelessly to mend the wounds of the Avignon Papacy and the schism, but the damage was too deep for quick and lasting healing. The crisis of the fourteenth century had produced a loss of respect for the pope and growing resentment in Christendom over the importance and role of the Roman church. Heretics used the crises to challenge orthodox teachings and advocate radical ideas, and their teachings gained a greater hearing because they attacked the ecclesiastical abuses of the day and exploited growing nationalist anomisity toward Rome.

The English scholar John Wyclif (1324–1384) dismissed the papal office as unnecessary for Church governance, advocated the supremacy of secular authority over the Church, and denied other basic Catholic doctrines. Wyclif's teachings were exported to Bohemia and influenced the priest Jan Hus, a popular preacher who attracted large audiences with his opposition to clerical corruption and immorality. Hus, too, challenged Catholic teaching on the papacy and denied several other central doctrines, and when he failed to heed episcopal condemnation of his heretical teachings, he was excommunicated by his archbishop. Eventually, he arrived at the Council of Constance to present the case for his heresy but was arrested and imprisoned. A trial was conducted at the council and Hus was declared a heretic and remanded to secular authority, who condemned and killed him at the stake. Hus's death sparked a nasty fifteen-year civil war in Bohemia that served as a small foretaste of the violence that would engulf Christendom a century later.

The general sentiment for most of the fourteenth century was that the popes in Avignon were nothing more than pawns of the French king. This was not accurate, but the residence of the popes in France and the occupation of the Chair of St. Peter by Frenchmen coupled with an overwhelming majority of French cardinals reinforced the sentiment. The amount of wealth required to support the papal bureaucracy, which grew in organization, stability, and power during the stay in Avignon, was immense, and many secular rulers and lay people believed that money was flowing out of their lands, especially England and German areas, to the benefit of their sworn enemy, France.[128] Thus in these dark times of the fourteenth-century papacy, that ostensible source of unity in the Church became the agent of disunity, instability, and corruption. The age of papal reform programs had passed; now it was the *papacy itself* that needed reform and renewal.

The events of the fourteenth century also laid the foundation for the subsequent great revolution against the Church and the shattering of Christian unity, the effects of which are still felt in the modern world. Despite the dark times, though, as happens with each crisis in Church history,

Christians did not lose hope or wallow in self-pity or cynicism. Instead, by God's grace the crises of the fourteenth century led to a spiritual renewal by the laity that served as the cornerstone for the later Catholic Reformation.

Renewal

During the tumultuous days of the fourteenth century, many Catholics who wanted to deepen their faith envisioned a return to the early days of the Church. In the Netherlands, an informal lay movement known as the *Confraternity* (or *Brethren*) *of Common Life* was started by Gerard Groote (1340–1384), who had studied medicine, theology, and canon law at the University of Paris. Though he was initially focused on worldly pursuits, a severe illness resulted in a conversion of heart and a deepening of Groote's faith. He entered a monastery and spent several years in monastic life until he left to become a missionary preacher. His popular preaching focused on virtuous living and attacks against the ecclesial abuses and clerical immorality of the day. Groote was ordained a deacon, but his preaching drew criticism, and he was silenced by his ordinary. A visit to the well-known mystic Bl. Jan van Ruysbruck (1293–1381) led to a decision, along with his friend Florentius Radewyns, to organize a community of laity dedicated to the pursuit of holiness. Groote died after contracting disease while ministering to plague victims but his community flourished.

The Confraternity was similar to the previous *Beguine* and *Beghard* movements in the eleventh-century Netherlands.

These groups of eremitical women and men, respectively, devoted themselves to prayer and good works, especially serving the poor. Members did not take vows and did not beg but rather sustained themselves through manual labor and teaching. The Beguines and Beghards sparked a religious revival in the thirteenth century, but lack of ecclesial oversight made the groups susceptible to heresy, leading to their condemnation at the Council of Vienne in the early fourteenth century. Now the Confraternity spread in the Netherlands and in German areas. Members did not take vows but lived in community oriented toward imitating the simple life of the early Christians. They wore humble clothing and limited the accumulation of possessions while spending time in prayer, listening to spiritual readings, and reading scriptural passages. Their spiritual life was known as the *devotio moderna*, which involved silent contemplation, self-denial, and meditation of Christ's Passion.[129]

The Confraternity was also dedicated to education and established schools with a curriculum focused on the liberal arts, philosophy, and theology. Members were known as excellent teachers and spiritual writers, and their numerous vernacular works were published and distributed throughout the Netherlands. The most famous work, published in the fifteenth century, was *The Imitation of Christ*, whose authorship is traditionally ascribed to Thomas à Kempis (1379–1471) but may have been Groote's. The spiritual work focused on the importance of authentic Christian belief lived in actual practice and exemplified the Confraternity's core teachings and way of life. Although education was a central work of the Confraternity, it was not an end in itself but rather one way in which to grow in faith, as reflected in the *Imitation*:

> What good does it do to speak in an educated way about the Trinity if your lack of humility displeases the Trinity? In fact, it is not education that makes a man holy and just, but a virtuous life makes him pleasing to God. I would rather feel contrition than know how to define it. For what would it profit us to know the whole Bible by heart, and the principles of all the philosophers, if we live without grace and the love of God? Vanity of vanities and all is vanity, except to love God and serve him alone."[130]

The crisis in the fourteenth-century papacy manifested a shift in the responsible agent of reform and renewal in the Church. Previous centuries highlighted the centrality of the papacy as the leading reform agent against ecclesial abuses, but in the wake of Avignon and the Great Western Schism the laity took up that task. Throughout Christendom, small lay groups arose with a desire to live the Christian faith authentically, free from the corruption and abuses prevalent within the hierarchy. Like-minded clerics assisted these lay men and women in the work of reform and renewal long before the papacy, during the Catholic Reformation, returned to its central role of ecclesial restoration. Most of the major religious orders, too, were stirred to reform and revival decades before the Council of Trent.

All these groups were marked by an embrace of the authentic nature of Catholic reform, which involves not a rejection of the authority of Christ's Church but the re-formation of the *self* in imitation of Christ. Only this self-reform, undertaken out of love of Christ and his Church, leads to general reform. No matter the century or the crisis of the day, this truth guides the faithful toward an authentic and fruitful response to the Church's ills.

7

The Renaissance Papacy and the Great Revolt

The new pope [Leo X] did not yield to the temptations of the flesh . . . His pontificate, however, demonstrates very clearly that when the cult of intelligence and beauty loses its sense of proportion and makes intellectual and artistic creations an end in themselves, it too constitutes a formidable spiritual temptation. The pope who builds the most splendid basilica in the world over the apostle's tomb but loses a quarter of his entire flock in the process, is surely carrying foolishness to the point of treachery.[131]

—Henri Daniel-Rops

THE DARKNESS:
A series of popes focused more on temporal matters than spiritual concerns distracted the Church's leadership at a time when strong leadership was required. As theological and political revolution fomented in northern Europe, the Church's leadership was distracted, which produced great division and separation of Christians.

THE LIGHT:
The cleaving of Christendom produced a great reform movement centered on the calling of an ecumenical council focused on the restatement of Catholic doctrine, the creation of vibrant new religious orders that carried the Gospel throughout the world, and the witness of holy men and women who produced a flowering of Catholic devotion and discipline.

Background

As the Church entered the fifteenth century, hope remained that the crises of the previous century would not return and that a new age of peace and tranquility would ensue. The pope again lived in Rome and the scandalous spectacle of three men claiming the papacy was over. The new century also witnessed a remarkable event that brought renewed optimism for joyous times ahead.

In the year that the Maid of Orléans was illegally executed based on false charges of heresy and for her role in freeing France from English clutches, Pope Martin V convoked an ecumenical council. It gathered initially in Basel but was eventually transferred twice: first to Ferrara and then to Florence, whence it takes its name. During the council, envoys from the Eastern Roman Empire arrived seeking reunion between the two halves of the Church. Faced with the dire threat of the Ottoman Turks, Emperor John VIII (r. 1425–1448) sought military assistance from the West and believed it forthcoming in exchange for reunification with Rome. The Byzantine envoys agreed to papal primacy and Pope Eugenius IV (r. 1431–1447) proclaimed the reunion on July 6, 1439.

However, the news was not greeted enthusiastically by many in the East, who still harbored deep animosity for the West and the pope for the sacking of Constantinople during the Fourth Crusade 200 years before. The reunion was indeed short-lived, as the Ottomans captured the Eastern imperial capital in 1453, ending the Roman Empire and solidifying the break between the two halves of the Church. The fall of Constantinople occurred during the pontificate of Nicholas V (r. 1447–1455) at a time when Europe and the Church were in the midst of the massive cultural expression and achievement known as the Renaissance.[132]

The Renaissance did not occur in a vacuum or spring up *ex nihilo* but was the product of the medieval world and the influence of the Church. Intellectuals in the fifteenth century focused on human activity with a special interest in ancient Greek and Roman manuscripts as well as a criticism of the established (i.e., Christian) order. Religious skepticism increased as intellectuals declared man to be the measure of all things and humanism became the focus of scholarly pursuits. Yet despite the reorientation of society away from God and toward man, the Church (particularly the popes) supported the great outpouring of artistic and architectural effort of the Renaissance, providing patronage and subject matter. The imitation of the ancients became a widespread pursuit of those in authority both secular and ecclesial.

Although the rich cultural movement of the Renaissance produced magnificent artistic achievements still visible and enjoyed today, the movement distracted the Church's hierarchy, who focused more on temporal pursuits than spiritual needs. The result was a papacy ill-equipped to effectively handle the theological and political revolutions that swept Christendom in the sixteenth century.

Crisis

Historians describe the popes from Nicholas V to Leo X as the time of the "Renaissance papacy." These ten popes, with pontificates spanning nearly seventy-five years, were guilty of various ecclesiastical abuses, including nepotism and pluralism (holding more than one diocese), and were focused more on temporal than spiritual affairs. Although the attention of popes for centuries had been held captive by the dictates of worldly affairs, due to their vast land holdings, these ten popes utterly cemented their attention on political concerns, truly acting more like secular princes than universal shepherds. Their behavior and activity coupled with the negative impacts from the fourteenth-century papal crises resulted in a papacy that "lost its universal pretensions and its universal position; it ceased, effectively, to be the head of Christendom, and became instead—and was generally regarded as—one of the Italian powers."[133]

The Renaissance popes weakened respect for the Petrine office not only from their political policies and military endeavors but also because of their personal behavior, little resembling the pre-Avignon saintly popes of recent memory. Indeed, the less disgraceful Renaissance popes were warriors and patrons of artists while the worst were despots and lechers.

The Dominican Tommaso Parentucelli was a lover of literature and a bibliophile. He studied at the University of Bologna where his brilliant mind and love of books drew the attention of Nicholas Albergati, the bishop of Bologna. Parentucelli spent decades working for the bishop, who was eventually created a cardinal, and attended the ecumenical council of Florence with him. When Bp. Albergati died in 1443, Parentucelli was chosen as his replacement and served dutifully for a number of years. Pope Eugenius IV died in 1447 and the cardinals then elected the scholarly Parentucelli as pope; he took the name Nicholas V (r. 1447–1455) in memory of his mentor and friend.

Pope Nicholas assumed the throne of Peter at a time of great political turmoil in Italy. The area was a patchwork of various kingdoms, duchies, and republics in the north and south with the Papal States sandwiched in the middle. Nicholas purposefully focused his papal agenda on Italian political issues but found time as well to patronize the arts in all forms—but especially literature and the collection of manuscripts. The first Renaissance pope moved the papal residence in Rome from the Lateran to the Vatican and began a concerted effort to collect Greek, Latin, and Hebrew manuscripts, which formed the genesis of the Vatican Library.

Nicholas died in the spring of 1455 and was replaced by the first Spanish pope, Alfonso de Borja (Borgia), who took the name Callistus III (r. 1455–1458). Callistus's pontificate was brief but filled with much activity. The pope tried to rally the forces of Europe to engage in a liberation of Constantinople from the Turks but to no avail. He also commissioned an inquiry into the trial and execution of the French warrior maiden Joan of Arc, which concluded after his death and resulted in Joan's rehabilitation. Callistus loved his family, especially his nephews, and utilized their loyalty in staffing curial offices. His short reign was followed by a true Renaissance man, Aeneas Sylvius Piccolomini, who took the name Pius II (r. 1458–1464). Ordained a priest later in life after decades in the service of clerics and the Church, as pope he focused his efforts on assembling a Crusade to liberate Constantinople and to calling Christendom to internal and external reform.

Pius believed that personal reform was a necessity in order to unite Christendom against the Turks. He sent invitations to the secular rulers of Europe to gather at Mantua in 1459 for a congress to discuss plans for the Crusade, but no one heeded his call. Undaunted, Pius continued efforts to raise the money and men needed for a military campaign to restore the former imperial capital to Christian control. The pope also pursued non-violent means to attain his goal when he sent a letter in 1461 to Mehmed II the Conqueror, the Ottoman sultan, urging his conversion to the Catholic faith; an exhortation that was ignored. Finally, Pius II decided to take the cross personally and lead the Crusade army, in hope that the sight of a frail old man embarking on a military campaign would shame secular rulers into action. He traveled to Ancona (central Italy on the Adriatic coast) in 1464 where the Crusaders assembled. But illness broke out among the troops and the sickly pontiff died, which ended the Crusade.

Pietro Barbo was elected as the successor to Pius II and took the name Paul II (r. 1464–1471). The nephew of Eugenius IV, Barbo entered the clerical state during his uncle's pontificate. Known for his love of parties, carnivals, and the arts, Paul II's pontificate was mostly uneventful. The next and fifth Renaissance pope became embroiled in a nasty political squabble with the powerful Florentine de' Medici family. Family was everything to Francesco della Rovere, who doted on his fifteen nephews, two of whom he created cardinal and one later became pope (Julius II). As Pope Sixtus IV (r. 1471–1484) he expanded the Vatican Library begun by Nicholas V and also commissioned the restoration of the old Cappella Magna chapel in the Vatican in 1477.[134]

But Sixtus's affinity for his family members tainted his pontifical achievements. His blatant nepotism was a regular source of criticism and blinded his judgment, especially in one incident in 1478. The Pazzi family, and others in Florence, was upset with the power of the de' Medici family and plotted to overthrow them. The conspiracy included a plan to assassinate Lorenzo the Magnificent and his brother Giuliano, the rulers of Florence, at Easter Mass in the cathedral. Sixtus IV's nephew was a conspirator, and the pope was aware of the assassination plot but urged his nephew to avoid bloodshed if possible. The attack resulted in Giuliano's death, but Lorenzo escaped with minor injuries. Other plotters attempted to gain control of the government, but the Florentine people sided with the de' Medicis, and many conspirators were killed. In the end, the failed coup only strengthened Lorenzo's power and sullied the reputation of the pope.

Giovanni Battista Cibò enjoyed worldly pursuits and pleasures as a young man, fathering two illegitimate children. However, he left his licentious ways and entered into the service of the Church, ordained a bishop in 1467 and created a cardinal the following year. When Sixtus IV died in 1484, Giovanni was elected in his stead and took the name Innocent VIII (r. 1484–1492). Innocent's pontificate was consumed with re-stocking the depleted papal treasury. Criticism abounded as the pope created new offices and other devious ways to increase revenue. The money-strapped pontiff even resorted to bestowing cardinalates on young boys, including the thirteen-year-old Giovanni de' Medici, although he was not allowed to assume the functions of the office until the age of sixteen. Innocent died in the summer of 1492 and was succeeded by the most infamous Renaissance pope, Alexander VI.

Rodrigo Borgia was a handsome, witty, learned, and eloquent man; personally charming, politically cunning, and thoroughly sensual. Created cardinal by his uncle Pope Callistus III in 1456, he was appointed to the influential, lucrative, and powerful posts of vice chancellor and commander of papal troops. Borgia used the prevailing ecclesial climate to his advantage by accumulating five wealthy dioceses. The Spaniard was also adept at navigating curial politics and exercised great influence in several papal elections. Borgia himself desired the papacy but was stymied in several attempts to acquire it. Eventually in the same year Columbus sailed to the New World, Borgia was elected pope, taking the name Alexander VI (r.1492–1503)—not to honor previous popes but in memory of Alexander the Great—and demonstrating his enthusiasm for the highest office in the Church by screaming, "I am pope! I am pope!"[135] At his election, Cardinal Giovanni de' Medici, who later became Pope Leo X, turned to a compatriot and said, "Flee! We are in the clutches of a wolf!"[136]

Before his papal election, Borgia lived a hedonistic life, taking several mistresses even as a cardinal. These liaisons resulted in children whom he openly acknowledged while pope, including a son, Cesare Borgia, who terrorized Italian towns and villages with a motley group of violent men. The author Niccolo Machiavelli accompanied Cesare on his rapacious romps and later wrote a book about political leadership titled *The Prince*, possibly modeled after the pope's bastard. When Alexander VI did not rebuke his rampaging son it produced scandal, but that reaction was a constant companion of the papacy. Even while pope, Alexander continued to enjoy the pleasures of the flesh, taking the beautiful nineteen-year-old Giulia Farnese as his mistress (the pope was in his sixties).

Political issues dominated Alexander's pontificate, especially the French invasion of Italy by Charles VIII in 1494, and much of his papacy was spent raising money, through simony, in order to fight wars and influence political affairs. Unsurprisingly, Alexander suffered severe criticism over his actions and policies during his life, especially from the fiery Florentine Dominican preacher Savonarola,[137] and by the end of his reign, Alexander had become the most famous Renaissance pope and the epitome of the ecclesial crisis of the age. When, in 1503 during the eleventh year of his pontificate, Alexander contracted a fever and died, Machiavelli summarized his pontificate and life well when he wrote, "The soul of the glorious Alexander was now borne among the choir of the blessed. Dancing attendance on him were his three devoted, favorite handmaidens: Cruelty, Simony, and Lechery."[138]

After the brief reign (twenty-six days) of Pius III (r. 1503), the cardinals gathered in conclave once more to elect the successor of St. Peter, choosing the nephew of Pope Sixtus IV, Giuliano della Rovere, who took the name Julius II (r. 1503–1513). In keeping with the age, the new pope was guilty of the abuse of pluralism, at one time holding the bishoprics of Avignon, Bologna, Lausanne, Coutances, Viviers, Mende, Ostia, Velletri along with the abbotship of two monasteries! Julius II was the personification of the Renaissance man, with a taste for art and architecture and having fathered three illegitimate children in his youth. Julius recognized the need for Church reform, and toward the end of his pontificate focused action in that area by convoking the Fifth Lateran Council in 1512.

His primary focus, however, was securing papal territory. Julius had inherited a messy political situation from his predecessors. Much of the territory of the Papal States had been lost during the French invasion of Charles VIII, and the papacy was in a precarious temporal position. Julius embarked on a series of military campaigns to restore the papacy's temporal power. Riding in full armor he led attacks against various Italian towns, prompting one contemporary to note that he "had nothing of the priest except the dress and the name."[139] The "warrior pope" succeeded on the battlefield and secured control of the Papal States for the next several centuries. His focus on military matters prompted Julius to ask the Swiss Diet in 1506 for a permanent corps of 200 mercenaries to form his personal bodyguard. Swiss soldiers were regarded as the bravest and most reliable fighting men in Europe and were sought after by rulers throughout Christendom.[140] Julius's *Swiss Guards* swore allegiance to the pope and were given the title "defenders of the liberty of the Church."

Apart from his military campaigns, Julius spent significant time and effort as a patron of artists and architects. He ordered multiple works of art and construction projects in Rome, including commissioning Raphael to paint the walls of the papal palace. Perhaps his most lasting artistic achievement was commissioning Michelangelo to adorn the ceiling of the Sistine Chapel with magnificent frescos. Emblematic of Julius's pontificate was his campaign to rebuild the basilica of St. Peter, which he initiated in 1506; though did not live to see its completion, as he died in 1513.

The last Renaissance pope was Giovanni de' Medici, the son of Lorenzo the Magnificent, ruler of the Florentine Republic. Giovanni was groomed from an early age for a life in the Church. He received the red hat at thirteen from Pope Innocent VIII and was only thirty-eight when elected pope. The death of Julius II brought division in the College of Cardinals, as one group favored an older, more experienced candidate and another favored Giovanni. Eventually, the votes swung in his favor and the young de' Medici was elected, taking the name Leo X (r. 1513–1521). Leo and his family were thrilled with the election. In a letter to his brother, the new pope wrote, "God has given us the papacy; let us use it to our advantage!"[141] Leo spent an exorbitant amount of funds maintaining the papal court and hosting extravagant parties and, like his predecessors, continued papal patronage of the arts while pursuing agendas oriented toward benefiting his family. The Fifth Lateran Council (1512–1517) completed its work during Leo's pontificate but the reform decrees passed at the council came too late for effective implementation. The powder keg of suppressed bitterness against the papacy, compounded by the fourteenth-century crises and the egregious actions of the Renaissance popes, exploded in a revolt in German lands that quickly dominated the last five years of Leo's pontificate and resulted in the most cataclysmic event in Church history: the cleaving of Christendom.

Christendom's health in the early sixteenth century was suspect. The Renaissance's focus on the human and temporal over the divine and eternal, coupled with previous political and spiritual crises, had taken a toll on societal morale. Questions concerning the role of the Church in society and its relationship with secular authority dominated discussion. Secular rulers no longer obeyed the pope or looked to the successor of St. Peter as a unifying force. The actions of the Renaissance popes fashioned and reinforced the belief that the Roman pontiff was more concerned about temporal than spiritual affairs, which produced indifference toward the papacy. Whereas in previous centuries the Church established universities, now secular rulers founded institutions of higher learning as separate entities from the Church. Kings became more independent of the Church while also seeking to make it an organ of their government. As Rudolf IV of Austria put it, "In my land, I will be pope, archbishop, bishop, archdeacon, dean."[142]

As kings sought greater governmental centralization, they clashed with papal efforts at ecclesial centralization.[143] Secular rulers were jealous of Church land and wealth and annoyed at the large sums sent to Rome to finance the papal curia. And of course, the weak leadership of the Renaissance popes, infected with nepotism, absenteeism, pluralism, and every vice, all sapped the vitality of the Church's salvific mission and fed new heresies—a point not missed in critical vernacular literature by authors such as Chaucer and Dante.[144] A writer named Herasmus Gerritszoon, known as Erasmus, exercised especially great influence over the perception of the Church. The son of a priest, Erasmus had entered an Augustinian monastery for a time but disliked monastic life and became instead an iterant scholar living off the proceeds of his writings. A witty satirist, Erasmus used comedy to highlight the corruption and abuses in the Church in an attempt to "tickle the Church into reforming itself."[145] Although Erasmus became a celebrated author and a sought-after member of secular courts, his attempts (and those of others) to push the Church away from impending disaster did not succeed. Instead, the wave of animosity toward the pope finally crested in the land of the Germans in the form of a dissatisfied Augustinian professor.

The Protestant movement in the sixteenth century, called the "Reformation," was in truth a religious *revolution*. Although social, cultural, and political factors were involved, the main issue was theological. It began "as a sort of spiritual family quarrel and continued as a spiritual civil war [but] was soon accompanied by an actual civil war in arms."[146] This great revolt against the Church succeeded in fracturing Christendom for a number of reasons, including the political constitution of German territory, resentment against Rome, military pressure by the Ottoman Turks on the borders of the Holy Roman Empire, and the avarice of the nobility.

In the sixteenth century, the area now known as Germany was a collection of nearly 400 small areas controlled by princes, dukes, and lesser nobility, along with a few free individual city-states all nominally led by the holy Roman emperor. Absent a strong national leader to serve as a counterbalance to the papacy, the mixture of dukedoms, principalities, and other governing entities was an area of competing interests into which resentment against foreign interference, especially the papacy, was cultivated and fueled by German nationalists. One such was the satirist Ulrich von Hutten (1488–1523), who painted the papacy as the enemy of the German people, writing:

> Three things are sold in Rome: Christ, the priesthood, and women. Three things are hateful to Rome: a general council, the reformation of the Church, and the opening of German eyes. Three ills I pray for Rome: pestilence, famine, and war. This be my trinity.[147]

Another contributing factor to the success of the great Protestant revolt was military pressure from the Ottoman Turks on the southern borders of the Holy Roman Empire during the early stages of the crisis. The situation consumed the attention of Emperor Charles V, who was unable to deal effectively and swiftly with the heretics and rabble-rousers. Protestants and their secular supporters used the military crisis to their advantage, effectively producing "a Christian mutiny during a Muslim invasion."[148]

The revolt was launched by the actions and writings of Martin Luther, a professor at the University of Wittenberg (sixty miles southwest of Berlin). Luther was a tortured soul who had entered the Augustinian monastery at Erfurt over the objections of his family, particularly his father who envisioned a lucrative legal career for his son, after surviving a terrifying storm on the way home from university. A brilliant student and diligent worker, Luther was obsessed with having knowledge of his own salvation and, despite living a sacramental life, could not obtain assurance of his justification before God. The young professor found solace in the study of St. Paul's epistle to the Romans, coming to believe that it was "faith alone" (*sola fidei*) that justified the sinner and assured one of salvation. He developed this theological notion through additional research and lectured on the topic to students, then soon embraced other heretical teachings concerning the authoritative form of divine revelation, human nature and the impact of original sin, and papal authority.

An opportunity to challenge Catholic teaching presented itself to Luther when the Dominican indulgence preacher Johann Tetzel arrived in German territory. Pope Julius II had granted a plenary indulgence in 1510 to anyone who contributed alms for the rebuilding of St. Peter's Basilica in

Rome. Pope Leo X continued the Julian practice, which led to Tetzel's preaching mission. Luther took umbrage at the practice of indulgence-preaching and in 1517 published his Ninety-Five Thesis questioning numerous Catholic practices and teachings. His work made its way to Rome, where it was reviewed and determined to be suspected of disseminating heresy. Luther was summoned to Rome to answer the charge in sixty days but refused to go, citing ill health. Pope Leo X sent Cardinal Thomas de Vio, also known as Cardinal Cajetan (from the Latinized version of his hometown Gaetano), to German territory to discuss the Ottoman Turkish threat and Cajetan was also ordered to meet with Luther and procure a repudiation of his heretical teachings and his reconciliation with the Church.

The meeting between the two men was not cordial and ended with violent outbursts of angry tempers. Luther later apologized to Cajetan for his behavior, on orders of his religious superior, but the damage was done to Luther's reputation in Rome. Nearly two years after publication of his famous treatise, Luther engaged in a disputation at Leipzig with the Catholic theologian Johann Eck. There, Eck masterfully exposed Luther as a Hussite heretic, after the Bohemian priest Jan Hus who had been executed at the Council of Constance in the early fifteenth century. A year later, Pope Leo X issued the bull *Exsurge Domine* in which forty-one of Luther's teachings were condemned and Luther was ordered to repent and submit to the Church's teachings within sixty days or suffer excommunication. Luther responded to the papal bull with an explosion of action and writing. He penned a reply to Leo's bull, titled *Against the Execrable Bull of Antichrist,* and conducted a public burning of *Exsurge Domine.* Later in the same year (1520) Luther published three treatises that solidified his heresy and laid the foundation for his revolutionary movement.[149]

As Luther's heretical and revolutionary teachings spread through German lands with the aid of the printing press and nationalist animus against the Church and papacy, after Luther was excommunicated by Leo X in January 1521 the holy Roman emperor, Charles V, decided to take action. Heresy was an ecclesiastical and secular crime, and since the Church had declared Luther a heretic, it was time for the secular authority to pass judgment as well. Charles invited Luther to the Diet at Worms in order to answer the charges against him and be afforded a last opportunity to recant his erroneous teachings. At the Diet, Luther refused to recant, and the devout Catholic emperor ruled that "it is certain that a single monk must err if he stands against the opinion of all Christendom. Otherwise, Christendom itself would have erred for more than a thousand years."[150] Charles V then declared the recalcitrant university professor a notorious heretic and subject to arrest, imprisonment, and death. But Luther had arrived at the Diet under imperial safe conduct and was allowed to leave under those promises as well. He was then "kidnapped" by forces loyal to his secular lord and protector, Elector Frederick of Saxony, and sheltered from imperial harassment for the rest of his life.

Luther's writing produced a spasm of violence throughout imperial territory, as attacks against the clergy and the Church, involving destruction of sacred art and the profanation of the Eucharist, soon gave way to a peasant rebellion. Concerned with the growing violence and societal disruption, members of the nobility asked Luther to utilize his voice to end the rebellion, since his writings, in part, were used by the peasants to justify their uprising. So the heretic published a clarion call titled *Against the Murderous, Thieving Hordes of Peasants* in which he exhorted the German nobles to violently quash the rebellion, which left more than 100,000 peasants dead. Over the next twenty years, German territory was split between Catholic (southern) and Lutheran (northern) lands as the great revolt tore asunder the peace and unity of Christendom. Luther died early in 1546 after writing one last treatise titled *Against the Pontificate at Rome, Founded by the Devil.*

The revolt did begin in German territory but did not stay there, spreading to other areas of Christendom and causing outbreaks of heresy and violence and a radical restructuring of society. A new revolutionary appeared in France and achieved success and fame in the Swiss town of Geneva. John Calvin (1509–1564) was very different from Martin Luther in all aspects of life. Luther was emotional, eloquent, irrational, rageful, and, at times, funny. Calvin was methodical, systematic, serious, intellectual, engaging, and humorless. A disaffected educated layman who embraced Protestant teachings learned at university rather than a scrupulous monk obsessed with his own salvation, Calvin had been a toddler when Luther published the Ninety-Five Theses.

When signs attacking the Mass appeared in Paris in 1534, King Francis I ordered a manhunt to find those responsible. Hundreds were arrested and several individuals were executed by the state for heresy, including some friends of Calvin. Recognizing it was no longer safe to hold heretical views in France, Calvin left and journeyed to Swiss territory. The following year, Calvin published the book that made him famous—in fact, it became the most widely read book of the sixteenth century. *Institutes of the Christian Religion* systematized Protestant theology, which up to that point had consisted of the jumbled mess of Luther's writings against the pope. Persuaded by fellow revolutionary Guillaume Farel to move to Geneva, Calvin became an important pastor in the town and ingratiated himself with the governing elite. The city had recently become a fully independent self-governing republic with a middle-class community protected by a fortified wall. Enthusiasts for the new Protestant movement had seized control of the city and by the time of Calvin's arrival, it had expunged all elements of the Catholic Church.

Calvin developed the Protestant movement in Geneva with his *Articles on the Organization of the Church and Its Worship.* All citizens were required to profess belief in Calvin's brand of theology or face excommunication. His vision for the city included theological overseers for each quarter of the city who would report to the ministers on the moral failings of each member under their purview. Needless to say, the *Articles* prompted great debate in Geneva. Anger swelled to the point of violence directed at Calvin, who responded by excommunicating the entire town on Easter Sunday 1538. The city council responded by ordering Calvin's exile the following day. The famous author had spent only eighteen months in Geneva before his unceremonious exit.

He traveled to Strasbourg, where he married and became pastor of a Protestant community. Political instability continued in Geneva for three years after Calvin's exile, but he still maintained supporters on the city council, and they successfully lobbied for his return, hoping that his forceful will could bring stability to the town. Calvin returned to Geneva in 1541 and began seizing full control of civil and ecclesiastical affairs. He incorporated the lessons learned from his previous failed attempt at establishing a theocracy in the *Articles* and developed a new plan in his *Ecclesiastical Ordnances*. Calvin instituted draconian measures rooted in his unflinching theological teachings, prompting the "war against joy."[151] Ministers and elders of Calvin's church visited each household in town twice a year to investigate adherence to Protestant teachings. Ledger entries were made for each person and recorded as *pious*, *lukewarm*, or *corrupt*. The death penalty was established for blasphemy, idolatry, heresy (from Calvin's teachings), offenses against chastity, and striking a parent. Prohibitions were enacted against dancing, singing (outside of church services), staging and attending plays, wearing jewelry, playing games of chance (dice and cards), wearing makeup, falling asleep during the sermon, and criticizing Calvin's theology. The teetotaling Calvin ordered the closure of all taverns in the city—though the violent reaction to the measure resulted in the reopening of five government-controlled taverns.

The theocratic society of Geneva did not produce the hoped-for idyllic "city on a hill," as there were frequent outbursts of opposition to Calvin's regime (all were forcefully quashed). Meanwhile, Calvin's teachings spread throughout Christendom from his frequent letters to other revolutionaries and from the establishment of the Geneva Academy, an institution of higher learning with enrollment mostly from outside Switzerland. Graduates of the academy returned to their home countries to foment rebellion and heresy. John Knox of Scotland spent time in Geneva and developed a friendship with Calvin. Knox returned to Scotland and was instrumental in ending the reign of Mary Stuart, Queen of Scots, and bringing down the local church. Calvin's devotees were sent into France, where a bloody civil war erupted that nearly ended the Catholic faith in the eldest daughter of the Church. Calvin died nearly twenty years after Luther, between the two of them having destroyed the unity of Western Christendom to this day.

Of course, there were other influential individuals and groups that participated in the revolt. The Swiss priest Ulrich Zwingli (1484–1531) rebelled against the Church and, despite his scandalous sexual immorality, convinced the town of Zürich to adopt his heretical teachings. He agreed with Luther on many theological points but also significantly differed from him, especially concerning the Eucharist. The two men disliked each other intensely and when Luther received news that Zwingli had perished on the battlefield against Catholic forces he remarked, "It is well that Zwingli lie dead on the battlefield. Oh, what a triumph this is, that [he has] perished. How well God knows his business."[152]

While Zwingli controlled Zürich, a dissident group of believers who rejected infant baptism and oath swearing and preached the near occurrence of the Second Coming, developed. Zwingli and his supporters mercilessly persecuted these "Anabaptists," so they were forced to leave the city. They eventually seized the city of Münster, removed all vestiges of the Catholic faith, confiscated all property, and decreed compulsory polygamy. Their activity was so radical that it united Catholics and Protestants in an army that liberated the city. Anabaptists were similarly arrested, imprisoned, and executed by secular authorities throughout Europe.

The Protestant movement produced a century of violence (1550–1650) in which war erupted in France, the Netherlands, and German territory, killing hundreds of thousands, and resulted in massive political and spiritual transformation. The Church's political influence, already waning, was severely curtailed and no longer recognized as a force in the public life of Europe. The Church was viewed as *a* church, not *the* Church. The papacy's influence on the political and spiritual life of Europe was likewise radically reduced.

Ecclesial authority was no longer acknowledged in the Church's hierarchy but rather placed in each individual believer, who could determine for himself how to interpret Scripture and develop Christian teaching.[153] The faith that Christ transmitted through the apostles, guarded by the teaching of the Church, now became subject to unchecked novelty and error in the lands where Protestantism took hold.

Although the most visible effects of the Protestant movement were corporate, there were also individual effects. The Reformation isolated the soul, diminishing the corporate quality of the Christian faith as lived in the society of Christendom.[154] Luther's heresy, with its focus on the individual, eroded Christian communion. A Christian looked no longer to the corporate authority of the Church for the truth, but rather to himself and his personal religious experience.

The logical extension of this individual focus results in a change in man's object of worship. Humanity is created to worship the Creator, but allowing for individual authority over the Creator's revelation leads to worship of man or self. Once any individual man becomes his own arbiter of revelation, revelation itself becomes something malleable, and then man rejects or becomes indifferent to revelation. A loss of authentic religion produces the worship of other things, including the state—which took monstrous forms in the twentieth century and produced horrific effects.

The theological revolution unleashed by Protestants also produced a change in worldview that led to the current secular culture of the West.[155] The medieval worldview was centered on the Church, and although Church and state were separate, and at times at odds with one another, society was united in a Christian foundation recognized by segments of the social order. The violence produced by the Protestant movement throughout Christendom, forced secular rulers to contemplate how to prevent such sectarian violence from repeating. The solution was the complete separation of religion from politics and the privatization of religious belief. Faith was no longer something common to society but was now the province of the private individual. This societal shift produced the concept of a subjective *rights-based* worldview rather than a worldview rooted in God-given objective truth. Citizens were provided the *right* to worship as they please by the state, or, in some rare cases (like the American experiment), civil government recognized the inherent religious right of citizens and guaranteed religion's free expression. The granting or recognition of religious expression to the individual from the government produces a separation of religion from the public sphere and lessens, or more appropriately, mutes the Church's influence in society. The consequences of that loss are profound with damaging effect on society and individuals.

Reeling from centuries of internal abuses, corruption, and complacency, the Church was racked by violent external forces in the Great Revolt. The crisis produced an acute situation and would have led to the demolition of the Church if it had been a purely human institution. Instead, motivated by the Holy Spirit, the Church entered into the Great

Reform, emerging from its greatest crises into a period of unparalleled renewal and vitality.

Renewal

From the wreckage of Christian disunity and the shattering of papal prestige came, incredibly, a papacy that was once again an agent of reform and renewal in the Church, as the Renaissance popes of the early sixteenth century gave way to the Reform popes later in the century. As in past reforms, the Catholic response to the Protestant revolt came to be centered on personal piety with an emphasis on prayer, living a sacramental and moral life, and a belief that the reformation of oneself would lead to the larger reformation of the Church as a whole.[156]

The tumultuous papacy of Clement VII (r. 1523–1534) saw the sacking of Rome by an imperial German army (with a large contingent of Lutheran troops) and the fall of England into schism in 1534 as King Henry VIII (r. 1509–1547), desiring to divorce Catherine of Aragon and marry Anne Boleyn, had an act of Parliament declare him the head of the Church in England. Upon Clement's death, the cardinals elected a seasoned veteran of the college as successor. Alessandro Farnese had been a cardinal for forty years and was unceremoniously known as "Cardinal Petticoat" because he was the brother of Giulia Farnese, Pope Alexander VI's mistress. The new pontiff was the oldest cardinal at sixty-seven when elected and looked frail and elderly with a long white beard, but he possessed a sharp mind with a strong character. In fact, despite his external appearance and age, Paul III (r. 1534–1549) produced the longest pontificate—fifteen years—in a century.

Although not considered a true Renaissance pope, Paul certainly lived like one. He appointed two grandsons to the College of Cardinals and a son, from a relationship prior to his pontificate, to the post of commander of the papal armies. Paul was an extremely popular pope with the Roman people due to ostentatious parties, bullfights, and horse races. He patronized Michelangelo and commissioned the artist to paint the famous Last Judgment fresco in the Sistine Chapel. Notwithstanding his ecclesial abuses and popular focus, though, Paul III initiated the Catholic Reformation and laid the foundation for the most comprehensive and successful renewal movement in Church history.

Paul conceived the Catholic Reformation in three stages. In his vision, the reform started at Rome with the papal court. The calling of an ecumenical council would follow the internal papal reform, and the final stage centered on the universal implementation of the reform council's decrees. Although recognition of the need for an ecumenical council was not lacking, planning the council proved problematic. Some major secular rulers were not supportive of the council or a strengthened Church. Nobility who had benefited from the confiscation of Church property feared that reconciliation would mean the return of stolen ecclesial treasure and their subsequent impoverishment. Notwithstanding the difficult situation and lukewarm secular support, Paul III called the council to meet at Mantua in the spring of 1537. Under the leadership of the Venetian Cardinal Gasparro Contarini, he established a reform commission that issued a report several months before the council's opening session.

The report, *De Emendanda Ecclesia*, placed blame for the Protestant revolt on the actions of the papacy, bishops, and clergy. It identified abuses of selling spiritual privileges, simony, pluralism, heretical teachings in universities, and poor intellectual formation of priests as particularly trouble-some and in need of eradication. The council was postponed in the summer of 1536 after war erupted between France and the Holy Roman Empire and the duke of Mantua informed the pope that he could not guarantee the safety of the assembly without additional military assistance. Paul III understood the request but feared the optics of a large body of armed men during the proceedings, so he postponed it until an alternative location was found. Vicenza, a city con-trolled by Venice, agreed to host the council in the spring of 1538, but when the papal legates arrived at the appointed start time only five bishops appeared, so Paul III suspended the council.

The need for reform and a response to Protestantism was still pressing, so when Holy Roman Emperor Charles V met with Pope Paul III in 1541, the emperor suggested a new location for the council: Trent. The town was geo-graphically well suited for the gathering since it was on the main road from German territory to Italy. Paul agreed, and issued the summons for the bishops to meet at Trent in

November 1542. However, when the papal legates arrived at the appointed time, again only a handful of bishops had assembled. The new year of 1543 witnessed the same paltry attendance and when war erupted between France and Charles V, Paul once more suspended the meeting. When hostilities ended in 1544, Paul issued another summons in the hope that the council would finally meet and begin its important work. That hope was met with success when the Council of Trent began in March 1545.

The task of the council was immense and consisted of defining and restating authentic Catholic doctrine in response to the heretical teachings of the Protestants as well as eradicating the abuses that contributed to the breaking of Christendom. Defining Catholic teaching was a necessity, since there had been no major theological statement from Rome on Protestant teachings since Leo X's 1520 *Exsurge Domine*. The task of eliminating ecclesiastical abuses was equally important, for a restatement of doctrine would prove futile without the conviction and dedication to holiness.

The council conducted its business over three general meetings spanning eighteen years from 1545 to 1563 and involved three pontificates (Paul III (d. 1549), Julius III (d. 1555), and Pius IV (d. 1565). Two lengthy suspensions due to the outbreak of plague (in 1547) and the presence of a Lutheran army near Trent (in 1552) delayed the conciliar work. At the first meeting (1545–1547), the Franciscan bishop and gifted orator Cornelio Musso gave the homily at the opening Mass and reminded his fellow bishops that the purpose of the gathering was "to defend the faith and the sacraments, to restore charity among Christians, [and] to eliminate from the body of the Church the poison of covetousness and ambition."[157] Procedures were established for the conduct of conciliar business, and doctrinal decrees concerning the role of Scripture and Tradition, the canon of Scripture, original sin and justification, as well as the sacraments of baptism and confirmation, were debated, voted on, and passed. Reform decrees banning the practices of absenteeism and pluralism were also approved.

During the four-year suspension of the council's work, Paul III died. His successor, Julius III, had been the senior papal legate at the first meeting of the council. He issued a bull summoning the bishops to reconvene in 1551 and continue the reform. This second meeting was brief, as the threat from a Protestant army marching near Trent forced another delay, but the council fathers were able to approve decrees on the sacraments of penance, extreme unction, and the Eucharist. But what was hoped would be a short delay in the conciliar work turned into a decade-long postponement and the death of another pontiff.

The third and final meeting of the council began in 1562 during the pontificate of Pius IV and was the most productive of all the gatherings. The well-attended sessions produced documents on the hierarchical structure of the Church, the religious life, purgatory, the saints and veneration of relics, the spiritual disciplines of excommunication and interdict, and indulgences. Recognizing the role that corrupt priests and bishops played in creating an atmosphere ripe for revolution, the conciliar fathers established reform measures focused on the clergy. In order to effectively form and train men for the clergy, the council required the establishment of a seminary in each diocese and defined minimum ages for diaconate and presbyteral ordination. Additionally, the fathers passed discipline canons aimed at the episcopacy. Bishops were required to reside in their diocese and could not be absent for more than three months—and never during the seasons of Advent and Lent. The shepherds of Christ were also exhorted to be attentive to the needs of their clergy and people, to preach each Sunday, to visit all the parishes in their diocese at least once a year, and to ordain only worthy and virtuous men to holy orders.

Finally, the council called for the revision and publication of the Roman Missal governing the celebration of Mass, the Breviary for the praying of the Divine Office, and a universal catechism for the teaching of the Faith. When Pope Pius IV closed the Council of Trent on December 4, 1563, it was a watershed moment in the history of the Church. In this new age in the Church's life, "the work of unification was at the same time a work of purification and rejuvenation. There was indeed, in 1563, a new Catholic Church, surer of her dogma, more worthy to govern souls, more conscious of her function and her duties."[158]

But although the decrees of ecumenical councils are important, they are meaningless unless implemented vigorously and unwaveringly by ecclesial leaders. Implementation of the decrees of Trent was accomplished by the energetic initiatives of Pope St. Pius V (r. 1566–1572), the establishment of the Society of Jesus, and the lives and actions of countless holy men and women.

Dominican Michele Cardinal Ghislieri seemed the perfect candidate to become the "father of the Catholic Reformation." Ghislieri was a pious man who ate and drank moderately, spent hours in prayer and meditation, especially upon the Passion of Christ, was devoted to the rosary, and served as the head of the Holy Office of the Roman Inquisition. Five days after his papal election in 1566, Pius V addressed the cardinals, exhorting them to personal reform by avoiding scandal. He firmly believed the clergy should lead by example and recognized that "we shall not paralyze the advance of heresy except by an operation proceeding from the heart of God. It is we, the light of the world, the salt of the earth, who must enlighten men's minds, enliven their hearts by the example of our holiness and our virtues."[159] Pius enforced his vision of a reformed clergy by creating virtuous men as cardinals, removing bishops guilty of heresy, and imprisoning those shepherds who refused to live in their diocese. Pius V rooted his pontificate in the implementation of the decrees of Trent and began in 1566 with the promulgation of the first universal catechism. A revised Breviary followed two years later and the issuance of a new Roman Missal followed in 1570. The work of this saintly pontiff produced a reinvigorated Church, a fighting Church that no longer shrank timidly from the damage wrought by the

Protestant movement but focused militantly on the tasks of reform and recovery and on missionary activity.

In the hindsight of history, it is not surprising that a soldier by profession should become the soldier of Christ who founded the Catholic Reformation's special forces. The military profession was embraced in Ignatius of Loyola's family—four of his brothers were soldiers—so Ignatius followed their example and fought against the French. When a severe wound that was not properly treated forced him to convalesce, Ignatius (1491–1556) underwent a profound spiritual conversion. Renouncing the military life, Ignatius lived as a hermit, practicing physical mortifications and spiritual meditations. His *Spiritual Exercises,* which he composed in his early thirties, offered a method for self-control and self-government rooted in prayer and examination of conscience. Several years later while studying in Paris, Ignatius formed the holy association of the Society of Jesus (Jesuits) along with six like-minded companions. Members of the Society pledged to live the evangelical counsels and to place themselves at the service of the Roman pontiff.[160] Pope Paul III approved the Society in 1540 and utilized the company of Jesuits in the work of the Great Reform.

The Jesuits focused their efforts for the Catholic Reformation on the sacraments, education, and missions. Realizing that education in the Faith was critical for the right living of the Faith, Jesuits placed an emphasis on catechesis as well as higher levels of learning. Their educational work manifested in the establishment and staffing of universities throughout Christendom. Missionary activity was an out-growth of their focus on education, and Jesuits famously journeyed the world spreading the Gospel to areas that had never heard it as well as areas that had embraced the Prot-estant heresy. St. Francis Xavier (1506–1552), one of the original companions of the Society, missioned to India, New Guinea, the Philippines, and Japan and died off the coast of China. When New France was established in the seventeenth century in North America, Jesuit missionaries arrived to spread the Gospel among the native peoples.

Eight members of the Society, including Sts. Jean de Brébeuf (1593–1649) and Isaac Jogues (1607–1647) were martyred by the Iroquois for their work among the Algon-quin and Huron peoples.[161] Their blood was the seed of new Christians, as a decade after the death of St. Isaac Jogues, in the same village of his martyrdom, a young girl was born of an Algonquin mother and Mohawk father. St. Kateri Tekawitha, the "Lilly of the Mohawks," gave compelling witness to her love for Christ throughout her brief life. St. Peter Claver (1581–1654) arrived in the New World and began a nearly half-century-long ministry to the African slaves brought to South America, despite the papal ban against such activity. In Europe, the Dutchman St. Peter Canisius (1521–1597) worked in Lutheran territory to bring former Catholics back into communion with the Church. He published several catechisms to assist in his work, founded numerous schools and colleges, and became known as the "second apostle of Germany."[162] The vigor of Jesuit faith and work advanced the task of the Catholic Reformation and ignited the fire of the Gospel in the Church in a manner not seen for centuries. And the Jesuits were not the only group dedicated to missionary activity during the Catholic Reformation: the Franciscans, too, were renewed through the actions of their holy missionaries across the ocean. Men like St. Junípero Serra (1713–1784) journeyed to the far reaches of the New World to establish missions, teach the native peoples, and celebrate the sacraments.

The Great Reform was buoyed by the actions of other holy men and women, too. Religious life found itself reformed and invigorated by the lives and work of the mystic St. Teresa of Ávila (1515–1582), who reformed the Carmelite order in Spain, and her compatriot St. John of the Cross (1542–1591), a great mystical writer and aesthetic who reformed the male Carmelites. Other reformers worked to implement the decrees of Trent. St. Charles Borromeo (1538–1584) became the first resident archbishop of Milan in nearly a century and worked tirelessly to reform and renew the clergy. He established schools and trained catechists to teach the Faith authentically. St. Philip Neri (1515–1595) focused his efforts on reforming souls through his personal example. He encouraged the Roman clergy and founded the Congregation of the Oratory as a community for priests to grow together in their faith and ministry.

One of the most effective missionaries to Protestants was Francis de Sales (1567–1622), who in 1594, only a year after his priestly ordination, volunteered to work in the Calvinist stronghold of Geneva and its environs. In 1602, he was ordained bishop of Geneva, but was forced to reside in Annecy, France since the Calvinist city would not allow the presence of a Catholic bishop. Francis wrote many tracts and pamphlets explaining the Catholic faith, provided catechetical instruction, and was renowned as a spiritual director. He propagated devotion to the Sacred Heart of Jesus and to guardian angels, and encouraged frequent reception of the Eucharist. His spiritual treatise, *Introduction to the Devout Life*, was well received and is still avidly read in the Church. Francis's love for the poor and his humble asceticism drew many Protestants to him; as a result, thousands of them came into the Church.

The efforts and prayers of these popes, missionaries, and saints all contributed to the massive renewal of Catholic life after the disaster of the Protestant revolution. The cleaving of Christendom became the impetus for the greatest reform in Church history. Weakened, beaten, and seemingly defeated, the Church recovered from the crises of the Renaissance papacy and the Protestant heresy and emerged transformed and girded by renewed devotion and discipline, which equipped it to endure unique obstacles and challenges as the modern world dawned.

When Pope Gregory XV (r. 1621–1623) canonized four saints who played critical roles in the Catholic Reformation, on the same day in May 1622, the Church was giving witness to its revival from the abuses, corruption, and scandalous behavior of previous centuries.[163] Indeed, the Church "had recovered all her fervor, all her hope; she no longer doubted the future, as she had once seemed tempted to do. Difficult days might come; the Word, of which she is the depository, would conquer, for she had been assured that the gates of hell would never prevail against her."[164]

8

The Enlightenment

The entire drama of salvation history had disappeared as far as the Enlightenment was concerned. Man remained alone: alone as creator of his own history and his own civilization; alone as one who decides what is good and what is bad, as one who would exist and operate even if there were no God.[165]

—Pope St. John Paul II

THE DARKNESS:
An insidious philosophy and worldview that rejected religion in general and the Catholic faith in particular swept through Europe. Proponents sought the destruction of the Church and its influence in the public arena.

THE LIGHT:
The Church, under the guidance of a holy pope, fought the rise of the nefarious ideology through targeted condemnations and reaffirmations of Christian truths about the role of faith and reason.

Background

The Great Reform not only responded to the Protestant revolt—it provided a foundation to withstand the attacks against faith and the Church during the modern age, beginning in the seventeenth century.

The vitality of Catholic institutions was sorely tested in this time of absolutist monarchs and revolutionaries. Advances in mathematics, physics, chemistry, physiology, geometry, and astronomy ushered in an era of "reason" that many trumpeted as the new post-Christian age[166]—even though the Church actually supported these advances and many of its members, especially Jesuit scientists, were key contributors to the increase in knowledge about the physical world.

For example, in the late sixteenth century, the Church instituted the Western world's first revision to the calendar since ancient Rome. The calculations underpinning the Julian calendar had been flawed, requiring an extra three days to be added to the calendar every four centuries. In order to correct the error and reestablish an accurate measure of time, Pope Gregory XIII (r. 1572–1585) established a commission led by the Jesuit Christopher Clavius. The commission developed a revision to the calendar that reduced the error to one day every 4,000 years, and its implementation was accomplished in October 1582.[167] The Church recognized the importance of understanding the natural world and encouraged scientists in their observations and research; it was wary, however, of attempts to utilize science to supplant or explain away supernatural teachings.

The Pisan Galileo Galilei (1564–1642) was a mathematician and astronomer who pushed the Church to embrace a scientific theory that challenged a centuries-old cosmology and threatened to impinge on doctrine. Galileo subscribed to the theory of *heliocentrism,* in which the Polish astronomer Nicholas Copernicus claimed that the sun was the center of the universe and not the earth (as in the prevailing Aristotelian-Ptolemaic *geocentrist* view). Heliocentrism was a controversial theory among scientists in the sixteenth century and was also disfavored by theologians, Catholics and Protestants alike, because some passages of Scripture seemed to justify geocentrism instead. But Galileo believed firmly in Copernicanism and advocated the theory in his 1610 work *Sidereus Nuncius* (*The Starry Messenger*).

In an effort to convince Church officials to support heliocentrism, Galileo traveled to Rome in 1615, despite admonitions from friends (both clerical and lay) to allow more research and time to definitively prove the theory. Galileo's discussions with Cardinal Orsini resulted in Pope Paul V (r. 1605–1621) referring the matter to the Roman Inquisition for study and judgment. The inquisitors were not sympathetic to a scientific theory that challenged the conventional theological interpretation of certain Old Testament passages suggesting geocentrism.[168] In an age where the Church's interpretation of Scripture was constantly opposed by Protestant revolutionaries, Galileo's request was probably an impossibility; nonetheless, he was extremely disappointed when the Roman Inquisition ruled heliocentrism to be "opposed to a doctrine which pertained to the faith according to the common consensus of learned theologians."[169] Though he did not get his wish, Galileo was told that he could continue research on the heliocentric theory—he just could not teach it publicly.

Galileo abided by the injunction of the Roman Inquisition for over a decade. But in 1632 he raised the issue again in his book *Dialogue Concerning Two Chief World Systems,* in which three fictional philosophers discussed the competing cosmologies. Galileo named the philosopher supporting the traditional geocentric cosmology *Simplicio* or "Simpleton" and placed in his mouth arguments in favor of the conventional view. Pope Urban VIII (r. 1623–1644) believed that some of *Simplicio's* comments imitated him, and the enraged pontiff established a commission to review Galileo's book. When it was determined that the scientist violated the previously issued injunction, he ordered Galileo to appear before the Inquisition. The aged astronomer complied, admitted his book was inappropriate, and publicly recanted his belief in heliocentrism. The Roman Inquisition placed Galileo's work on its Index of Prohibited Books and imposed a penance on the contrite scientist. Galileo lived peacefully for another nine years.

In later centuries, modern secularists fostered a false narrative about Galileo's research and interactions with the Church in order to paint Catholicism as the enemy of scientific achievement and human advancement. This lingering modern belief that the Church is opposed to science stems from the writings and thoughts of anti-Catholic and anti-religion Enlightenment authors who wanted to diminish the influence of religion in society. These Enlightenment intellectuals fantasized that Galileo "groaned away his days in the dungeons of the Inquisition, because he had demonstrated by irrefutable proofs the motion of the earth."[170] This false characterization of the Galileo affair makes him a "martyr for intellectual and scientific freedom" against a backward and superstitious Church; but the reality is far more complicated, and it was driven in no small part by the arrogance and duplicity of Galileo himself. As the eminent Catholic scientist Fr. Stanley Jaki observed, Galileo, "though not plagued with a martyr complex, considered himself a martyr without seeing that he was largely responsible for bringing martyrdom upon himself."[171]

These modern myths born in the Enlightenment also assert that the reason the Church is opposed to science is because science is a rival—providing answers to questions long believed answerable only by faith, making religion, especially the Catholic Church, irrelevant. This notion is rooted in the belief that great advances in science arose in a "scientific revolution" that erupted only once the power of the Church was destroyed. But although there were significant advances in many scientific fields during the sixteenth and seventeenth centuries, these developments were produced mostly by faithful Christian scholars, based in Christian universities, whose successes were built on the backs of Catholic scholars over the previous centuries.[172] And they were developed in a philosophical milieu that accepted the general stability of the physical world and the general reliability of the senses in discovering reality—without which, science simply can't happen.

Far from serving an explosion of science, then the philosophical movements of the Enlightenment period threatened it, for whereas Catholic philosophy was rooted in reality and principles of reasoning based on observation, "enlightened" philosophers questioned whether anything could be known with certainty. In an effort to bring certitude to philosophical questions concerning knowledge and the existence of God, the Frenchman René Descartes (1596–1650) developed a methodology in which thinking became the determinant of existence.[173] Unintended but inevitable consequences of Descartes's rationalism were skepticism and moral relativism, since by it each individual is invested with the authority to make personal determinations on reality and existence, including right and wrong.

Throughout the era, this fundamental shift in human reasoning entered all forms of intellectual pursuits and reinforced earlier movements toward a man-centered society that rejected God and the Church. "Enlightened" teachings posited a worldview rooted in empiricism and materialism to the detriment of the spiritual and supernatural. The divorce of philosophy from objective reality initiated, in subsequent centuries, a savage attack on the Church and the faithful. Enlightened thinkers hated religion generally and the Catholic Church especially. They believed that the Church's doctrine was unreasonable and its authority smothering. Thoroughly secularized leaders dominated governments and created a modern nation-state that demanded total obedience—and tolerated no rivalry from the Church in the public square.

Following the success of the Great Reform, and as the modern world dawned, the political and ecclesial crises facing the Church were in some ways unimaginable. But they would lead to unprecedented violence, death, and destruction.

Crisis

Enlightenment thinkers realized that if their method of reason and their hatred of the Church were to take permanent root in society, they needed to control the centers of higher learning, the universities, which, at the time, were dominated by the Jesuits. The subsequent assault on the Society of Jesus, the bedrock organization of the Catholic Reformation, began with the writings of François-Marie Arouet, known by the pen name Voltaire (1694–1778). Although educated by the Jesuits, Voltaire came to embrace Enlightenment ideas and ridiculed the Church. He knew that the influence of the Jesuits rested in their educational system. The Society was an obstacle to inculcating modern secular ideas in the minds of Europeans, so Voltaire targeted his gifts and influences on the task of extinguishing the religious order. In 1773 he wrote, "Once we have destroyed the Jesuits, we shall have our own way with the infamous thing [the Church]. [When the Jesuits are suppressed] in twenty years there will be nothing left of the Church."[174]

Secular rulers bent on absolutist control in their kingdoms disliked the Jesuits because their special loyalty to the Roman pontiff presented a strong obstacle to central state authority. Additionally, their defense of indigenous people in the New World colonies was angering many colonial nations. The attack against the Society began in Portugal where the Marquis de Pombal, the chief minister of King Joseph (r. 1750–1777), began a propaganda campaign against the Jesuits and convinced the king to expel the group from Portugal and Brazil in 1755. Next, the Jesuits were persecuted in France, where they were not allowed to teach theology and their schools were closed. Eventually, King Louis XV (r. 1715–1774) expelled the Jesuits entirely from France and all its dominions. The Jesuits were expelled also from Spain—birthplace of their founder St. Ignatius—and its territories in April 1767.

The intense pressure on the popes by secular European powers to suppress the Society reached its apex with the death of Clement XIII (r. 1758–1769). During his pontificate, the pro-Jesuit Clement XIII fought against the persecution of the Society, even releasing the bull *Apostolicum pascendi* in support. However, his death brought opportunity to the secularists. When the cardinals met in conclave to elect the papal successor, they were met with formal requests to suppress the Society from the nations who had already expelled the Jesuits from their territories. The cardinals divided into groups of those arguing in favor of suppression and those who demanded steadfastness. The new pope, Clement XIV (r. 1769–1774), was a Conventual Franciscan who had been educated by Jesuits, and he agonized over the situation. He delayed a decision for the first few years of his pontificate but, eventually, the pressure became too great to postpone the action any further.

So, on July 21, 1773, Clement XIV promulgated the document *Dominus ac Redemptor*, which suppressed the Society of Jesus universally. Clement believed the Church would not be at peace with the powers of Europe as long as the Society of Jesus existed. Clement XIV hinted at other reasons for the Society's suppression in his document but did not delineate them, merely writing that "forced by other motives which prudence and good government of the Church have dictated; the knowledge of which we reserve to ourselves; [and] after a mature deliberation, we . . . suppress and abolish the said company."[175]

Clement's action, undertaken to pacify increasing belligerent rulers, was a shocking decision that marked a watershed moment in Church history. The main proponents of the Great Reform, the order that produced missionary martyrs in the Old and New Worlds and militantly assisted in a renewed Catholic vitality after a period of disunity, despair, and drudgery, had been summarily written out of existence. The disgraceful decision has not been forgotten by the successors of St. Peter, who have refused to take the name Clement since.[176]

The suppression of the Society of Jesus allowed secular rulers and other political elements in European society the opportunity for greater governmental control, which further weakened the Church's influence. France, the eldest daughter of the Church, faced a shattering of its political and religious institutions. Toward the end of the eighteenth century, the Church in France had appeared in a strong and stable position. Nearly 100 percent of the population was Catholic and the Church owned ten percent of all land.[177] The monarchy had been personally devoted to the Faith and a supporter of the Church. Despite the seemingly favorable conditions, the Church in France at the end of that century was facing its "first intellectual and armed challenge since the Great Persecution launched by Roman emperor Diocletian."[178]

France achieved a great victory over England, its longtime rival, in the American War of Independence (1775–1783), where French military assistance to the rebellious English colonists proved decisive at Yorktown in 1781. But the long and costly war had run the nation into debt from which it could not recover. Indeed, by the late 1780s, half the royal budget was spent on servicing the interest on loans.[179] Enemies of the Church believed that the financial crisis could be solved by usurping the wealth and property of the Church, as had been done in the Protestant nations of Europe. King Louis XVI (r. 1774–1792) disagreed with the anti-Church opinion but knew something radical must occur for the nation to recover. So, he called a meeting of the *Estates-General*, a representative advisory body that had not convened in 175 years,[180] and eventually conflict among the common people led to the creation of a National Assembly tasked with crafting a national constitution.

Then, in the summer of 1789, revolutionary elements in Paris stormed the Bastille, a medieval fortress turned royal prison that had become a symbol of supposed oppression by the monarchy.[181] These actions initiated one of history's most catastrophic political and religious revolutions, whose advocates saw two main obstacles to victory: the monarchy and the Church. Over the next four years they would eradicate one and grievously harm the other.

After the revolutionaries seized control in 1789, they imprisoned the royal family in the Tuileries Palace. Less than two years later, Louis, Marie-Antoinette, and their children attempted to escape to the frontier, but were arrested and brought back to Paris. In the summer of 1792, an armed mob descended on the Tuileries and took the king and queen into custody after a heroic but futile stand that took the lives of more than 600 Swiss Guards.[182] A month later the monarchy was officially abolished.

While the king was incarcerated, the revolutionaries attacked the Church: confiscating its lands in November 1789, then suppressing religious orders and closing some churches. On July 12, 1790, the revolutionary government enacted the Civil Constitution of the Clergy, which officially separated the Church in France from Rome and initiated government control over it. People were to elect their bishops, diocesan boundaries were redrawn to match civil jurisdictions, clergy were considered employees of the state and required to take an oath of fidelity to the government. The following year in September 1791, the National Assembly was disbanded and replaced with the Legislative Assembly, with no ecclesial participation or representation allowed. In 1792, the Legislative Assembly was replaced by the Committee of Public Safety, which launched the Reign of Terror.

The terror began when radicals took control of Paris and went on a killing spree that murdered hundreds of bishops, priests, and religious in one day for refusing to take the oath required in the Civil Constitution of the Clergy. The following year witnessed the height of the terror, which included the execution of Louis XVI in January and Marie-Antoinette in October. The spasm of violence continued alongside an intensified de-Christianization campaign to rid France of its Catholic culture and history. The Gregorian calendar was changed to a "calendar of reason" with new names for the months and a new ten-day week, in order to abolish Sunday as the day of worship. The calendar now comprised ten months of three weeks with every tenth day as a period of rest. Churches were confiscated and turned into "temples of reason" and a prostitute was crowned "goddess of reason" in Notre Dame cathedral.

In the Vendée region of southwest France, a Catholic uprising against the anti-Christian revolutionary forces erupted from March to December 1793. The troops from the Vendée marched into battle under the banner of the Sacred Heart of Jesus, and if not for a sniper's well-placed shot that killed the leader, the movement might have succeeded in stopping the revolution. As it happened, though, the failure of the uprising resulted in even more severe measures, as the government committed genocide of the Catholic people of the Vendée, killing hundreds of thousands.[183]

The Reign of Terror came to an end in 1794, in part due to the heroic martyrdom of sixteen Carmelite nuns who gave their lives as holocausts for an end to the killing. The next year witnessed the establishment of another governmental body, the Directory, which sought to craft some semblance of organized government again. However, the violence continued with riots in Paris, so the Directory called upon a young artillery officer named Napoleon Bonaparte to restore order. Napoleon's successful leadership in the riot soon won for himself greater power and authority. In 1798, he led a successful military campaign to Italy, which resulted in the conquest of Rome and the arrest of Pope Pius VI (r. 1775–1799). The pontiff was forcibly brought to France, where he died in captivity, and mockingly declared "Pius the Last" by Napoleon. However, Christ promised that the gates of hell would not prevail against the Church, so the cardinals assembled in Venice and elected Barnaba Chiaramonti, who took the papal name Pius VII (r. 1800–1823). A year later, the French government and the Church entered into a concordat that brought peace and stability, seemingly, after the many years of violence and persecution.

Napoleon's thirst for power culminated in his coronation in 1804 as emperor, and his desire for world conquest led him once more to Italy where he annexed the Papal States to the French Empire, an action that led to his excommunication by Pius VII. In response, the Corsican despot kidnapped the pope and brought him to France, where he stayed in exile for six years. Eventually, the threatened European powers banded together to defeat Napoleon twice, the second time on the battlefield at Waterloo, which led to his own final exile.

In the following century, the political upheaval in France swept the rest of Europe in similar fashion, along with unprecedented societal transformation as the Industrial Revolution began changing European society from an agrarian to an urban culture. Although positive in many aspects, the Industrial Revolution radically altered traditional family life as men, women, and children worked long hours in factories and lived in tight concentration with others in cities. Population swelled in Europe and large numbers of immigrants left its shores seeking fortunes in distant lands. At mid-century, nearly every nation was suffering from political mayhem as socialist-inspired revolutions swept through continental Europe. The political upheaval produced changes in governments and inspired secular nationalist groups in Italy to clamor for an end to the Church's ancient temporal land holdings in order to bring about Italian unification.

Renewal

In the midst of significant upheaval and persecuted by Enlightened secular rulers, the Church was graced with a vibrant and resolute Roman pontiff. When Giovanni Mastai-Feretti was elected pope in 1846, taking the name Pius IX (r. 1846–1878), he could not have anticipated the cataclysmic shift in papal authority during his reign. Perhaps it was providential that he was the youngest pope (fifty-two) in centuries, as his youth and vigor served him well in the troubles that dominated his pontificate. Two years into his papal reign, political revolutions swept throughout Europe. Riots broke out in Rome and a gruesome scene occurred on November 15, 1848, a night that remained in Pius's memory. Count Pellegrino Rossi, prime minister of Rome, was murdered in the presence of the pope and other dignitaries when a revolutionary infiltrated the gathering and slashed Rossi's neck with a knife. Blood sprayed the crowd and landed on Pius IX.[184] Soon thereafter, mobs formed outside the Quirinal Palace (the papal residence) demanding democratic reforms in the Papal States. The pope refused to acquiesce to the mob and shots were fired into the palace, killing the papal secretary.

Recognizing that the situation was unstable and dangerous, Pius left Rome for the safety of Naples dressed in disguise as an ordinary priest, carrying the Blessed Sacrament in the same ciborium taken by Pius VII to France when captured by Napoleon years early.[185] In Naples for the next two years, the pope requested the intervention of Catholic secular rulers in order to establish and maintain order in Rome, and French troops came to occupy the city as a security force in the summer of 1849 (they would stay until 1870). Pius returned to the Eternal City in 1850, compelled by what he had undergone to reject modern liberalism and its democratic principles.

His pontificate continued to suffer from political troubles as Italian nationalists grew in strength and demanded the eradication of the Papal States. When French troops left Rome in 1870 to defend their homeland against Prussian aggression at the start of the Franco-Prussian War, nationalist supporters invaded papal territory and absorbed it into the new unified nation of Italy. The thousand-year-old papal territory ceased to exist outside of the Vatican, where Pius declared himself a "prisoner" and refused to leave for the remainder of his long pontificate. In recognition of the unjust action against the Church, Pius withheld the traditional *Urbi et Orbi* (to the city and the world) solemn blessing for the rest of his pontificate.

Recognizing the threat posed by the Enlightenment and its dominant secular and anti-religious worldview, Pope Pius IX promulgated the document *Quanta Cura* in 1864. The document contained a *Syllabus of Errors*, a condemnation of eighty heretical theological, philosophical, and political propositions, such as pantheism, atheism, indifferentism (the belief that all religions are the same), and communism. The Church's post-Enlightenment experience in France and Italy convinced its leaders that modern philosophy and secular governments were threats to the Christian faith. The idealized goals of the French revolutionaries—"Liberty, Equality, Fraternity"—meant for the Church "atheism, persecution, and eradication." The Church became wary of new governmental structures imbued with Enlightenment principles and sought its protection and independence in a strong centralized Roman curia under the leadership of the pope.

Although papal writings could express the Church's rejection of Enlightenment ideals and condemnation of nefarious political ideologies, Pius IX recognized the need for an ecumenical council, the first since the great council at Trent, to place the Church on a renewed foundation truly strong enough to withstand the assaults of the modern world. The First Vatican Council opened on December 8, 1869 and met for only seven months due to the outbreak of the Franco-Prussian War, but it produced documents on faith and reason and on papal primacy and infallibility. The conciliar document *Dei Filius* was a response to the errors of the Enlightenment and a "restatement of the fundamental truths of the Christian religion against the new rationalism."[186] *Dei Filius* affirmed Catholic doctrine that truth is a gift from God and that the truth can be known by human reason. Additionally, the document re-stated Catholic belief that faith and reason are complimentary, not opposed as advocated by Enlightenment ideologues, because God is the author of both.

The council's document on papal primacy and infallibility, *Pastor Aeternus*, was meant to encompass a discussion on the Church as a whole, but its work was interrupted by political events, and *Pastor Aeternus* was limited explicating Catholic teaching on the role and jurisdiction of the Roman pontiff. Recognizing Jesus' establishment of the Church upon Peter, the council taught that Peter and his successors received true primacy of jurisdiction in the Church. Additionally, *Pastor Aeternus* taught that Christ gave Peter and his successors the keys of heaven and earth and their concomitant authority, which included the unique charism of *infallibility;* so that when the Roman pontiff teaches on a matter of faith and morals as the universal shepherd of the Church on a matter to be held definitively by the faithful, that teaching is preserved from the possibility of error.

The discussion of and teaching on papal infallibility was not on the conciliar agenda originally and was heavily debated by the bishops, especially from the areas of Europe most infected by Enlightenment ideas. Hesitant bishops did not disagree with the doctrinal teaching on papal infallibility itself but rather on its presentation and inclusion in the document. Some believed that the teaching would prove a stumbling block in relations with the Orthodox and Protestants and viewed it as a push to centralize Church governance from Rome. Other bishops argued the teaching would antagonize the secular governments of Europe, who wanted to control the Church within their borders, and feared it would incite greater persecution. In the end, the bishops voted by a large margin to accept the teaching, even though the belief that persecution from it was in the offing proved prophetic. And even though war permanently interrupted the council, its brief work provided the Church with a needed doctrinal statement against some of the main errors of the Enlightenment.

The efforts of Bl. Pius IX resisting anti-Catholic political forces and the work of the First Vatican Council in condemning erroneous Enlightenment teachings renewed the Church by reiterating Catholic teaching and establishing clear boundaries between Church and state. However, soon after the council's conclusion, the Church was faced with an attack against both teaching and boundaries in Germany, where secular nationalist forces imbued with Enlightenment principles began a fierce campaign of persecution. Toward the end of the nineteenth century a new united German Empire had come into existence under Prussian leadership. Otto von Bismarck (1815–1898), the first chancellor of the new nation, desired to fully unite the German people in a shared culture and religion and believed the Catholic Church was an obstacle to that dream. Bismarck initiated a fifteen-year *Kulturkampf* or "culture war" against the Church.

The "iron chancellor" viewed the pope as a foreign ruler who should not exercise any influence in the new country, and used the document *Pastor Aeternus* as proof that the pope sought control over the nations of Europe, stating, "It is the infallible pope who threatens the state! He arrogates to himself whatever secular rights he pleases . . . in a word, no one in Prussia is so powerful as this foreigner."[187] Following up on such rhetoric, Bismarck enacted anti-Catholic laws and persecutory measures to isolate the Church in Germany from Rome. The 1871 Pulpit Law imposed severe penalties on any clergy member who criticized the government in a homily. Laws forbidding religious instruction in schools, requiring government approval of ecclesial appointments, and refusing to legally recognize Catholic marriages celebrated in the parish were also implemented. Outright persecution erupted also as bishops and priests were arrested and imprisoned, monasteries closed, Church land and schools seized, and diplomatic relations with the Vatican severed.

German Catholics resisted these measures non-violently and formed the political Center Party, which won seats in the Reichstag in the 1874 national elections. Pius IX addressed the untenable situation in Germany with the encyclical *Quod nunquam* and declared the anti-Catholic laws invalid. Eventually, the *Kulturkampf* ended with a diplomatic accommodation between Bismarck and Pope Leo XIII (r. 1878–1903) but the impact on Catholic life in Germany lingered.

At the end of the nineteenth century, the Church had survived the surge of the Enlightenment and the rise of anti-Catholic secular governments in Europe. And even the loss of the Papal States, seen at the time as a devastating attack on the Church, proved providential, as a papacy relieved of temporal concerns for ecclesial land holdings could now focus on continued spiritual renewal and provide a bulwark against future secular persecution in the new century.

9
———

Modernism and Neo-Paganism

The future to envisage is a pagan future, and a future pagan with a new and repulsive form of paganism, but nonetheless powerful and omnipresent for all its repulsiveness. [But] reaction there will always be and there is about Catholic reaction a certain vitality, a certain way of appearing with unexpected force through new men and new organizations.[188]

—Hilaire Belloc

THE DARKNESS:
Modern nation-states embraced radical political ideologies, utilitarian in nature, that subjected the individual to the state, while a sinister heresy invaded the Church and the world, leading to skepticism and moral relativism.

THE LIGHT:
In the darkness, light shines on the Catholic laity, called to duty by an ecumenical council and driven by a desire to renew and reform the Church through vibrant new means of evangelization and catechesis.

Background

As the twentieth century dawned, a pernicious heresy known as *Modernism* attacked the Faith from within, seeking to undermine the supernatural underpinnings of the Church's doctrine by, for one example, positing purely natural explanations for the miraculous. Unlike previous heresies that questioned specific dogmas and doctrines, Modernism opposed the very meaning of all those teachings. The heresy took root in biblical scholarship but also infiltrated other disciplines, producing a subtle denial of divine revelation along with a desire to erase the influence of the Church in temporal affairs. A Modernist society, the fruit of Cartesian thought, produces skepticism and moral relativism, making morality a construct of humanity rather than a plan from God for eternal happiness. The resulting rejection of Christian ethics tends toward a new form of paganism rooted in the acceptance of vile and repulsive individual and communal behavior, to the detriment of society and the Church.

The Church condemned the evils of Modernism in its nascent form in the late nineteenth century during the pontificate of Pope Bl. Pius IX, but it was in the early twentieth century where the Church focused its efforts on this malignancy. After the twenty-five-year pontifi-cate of Pope Leo XIII (r. 1878–1903), the cardinals elected Giuseppe Melchiorre Sarto, who took the name Pius X (r. 1903–1914). A consummate pastor of souls, Pius X was gravely concerned about the spread of Modernism and its influence on institutions of higher learning. So, in July 1907, in the encyclical *Lamentabili,* Pius condemned sixty-five Modernist errors; later that same year, he issued *Pascendi Dominici Gregis* concerning the errors of Modernism, which he called "the synthesis of all heresies." Additionally, Pius X required all professors at pontifical institutions to take an oath against Modernism and to teach faithfully the Church's doctrines. But although these documents and the oath assisted in fighting the heresy, the Modernist crisis remained a critical issue for the Church through the rest of the twentieth century.

Crisis

Modernism produced violence on an unparalleled scale and the establishment of a post-Christian worldview. Its fruits were on full display early in the twentieth century when a tragic, yet seemingly isolated event, occurred in the summer of 1914 in Sarajevo. The heir to the Austro-Hungarian Empire, Archduke Franz Ferdinand and his wife Sophie were brutally gunned down by a Serbian revolu-tionary. Distraught at the death of his beloved nephew, the aged emperor Franz Josef issued an ultimatum to Serbia, which amounted to an Austrian takeover of the country.

The Serbians rejected the emperor's demand, and so Austria declared war on its comparatively tiny neighbor.

Imbued with the fruits of the Enlightenment, European nations focused on nationalistic and worldly ambitions through the late nineteenth and early twentieth centuries. A grand contest for control of natural resources and the establishment of overseas colonies consumed the major European powers. These nationalist ambitions drove the creation of large standing armies and the misguided patriotic impulse to use them. The summer of 1914 gave these powers the chance to flex their nationalist ambitions on the Continent itself.

Politically, Europe was enmeshed in a collection of alliances that automatically triggered the mobilization of armies if certain conditions were met. The Russians were allied with Serbia, and so Tsar Nicholas II had no choice but to order his army's mobilization. This triggered a reaction in Germany, which mobilized its troops and planned for the invasion of Belgium in order to avoid French border defenses and then make a sweeping turn into the heart of France in the hopes of capturing Paris and knocking the French out of the war quickly. The Germans knew that Great Britain would enter the war as a result. In the quick span of five weeks, all of Christian Europe had mobilized for the "war to end all wars."

The First World War (1914–1918) did not end war but it did bring battlefield casualties in numbers never seen in human history. After making advances into Belgium and France, the Germans were stopped and all sides on the

Western Front dug defensive trenches, stretching for a thousand miles. Neither side was able to break the stalemate, even with the advent of new weapons such as the tank and airplane, and years of staggering death tolls and gains measured in inches resulted. In the first three weeks of the war, more than a million men were killed, wounded, or missing; in 1915, more than four million; in 1916, more than two million on the Western Front alone.[189] The impact on Germany was immense, as nearly one-third of all German males were killed, maimed, or incapacitated by illness or injury as a result of the war.[190]

The Church did not remain silent while the nations of Europe, mad with Modernist empiricism and rationalism, wasted lives for political gain. Pope Benedict XV (r. 1914–1922) was elected to the papacy at the very beginning of the war, on September 2, 1914. A trained diplomat from Genoa, he had served as undersecretary of state for Leo XIII and Pius X and had been created a cardinal only three months before his papal election. Benedict decided to abide by three principles during the war: perfect neutrality, extension of charity to all victims of the war, and calling for peace at every opportunity. (Pope Pius XII would also adopt these principles when the next great war erupted later in the century.) Benedict pursued neutrality because it allowed the Church to remain above the political disputes even though this position angered both sides of the conflict. It also allowed the Church to be a voice of reason, calling on both sides to conduct their wartime actions in accordance with the moral law. When that did not occur, the pope was able to lodge public and private protests concerning the conduct of the combatants.

The pope was especially concerned with the impact of the war on families, so he created the Prisoners of War Bureau, which facilitated communication between POWs and their families. The Vatican also crafted prisoner exchanges, especially for wounded soldiers and fathers of three or more children. The pope never stopped calling for peace throughout the conflict, urging an end to hostilities, a reduction in armaments, respect for the freedom of the seas, and the settling of disputes by international arbitration. After the war ended on the feast day of St. Martin of Tours, November 11, 1918, the pope exhorted the victors to make peace without demanding reparations from Germany. Unfortunately, they refused to listen and created the Treaty of Versailles, the severe terms of which humiliated Germany and laid the foundation for another world war.

In the midst of the world war and especially its aftermath, the political ideologies of communism, National Socialism, and fascism began to poison the Western world. These political systems appeared to be at odds but they shared the animating belief that the individual was subservient to the state. As the ideologies took root in numerous countries, their leaders and supporters sought to discredit and limit the temporal and spiritual authority of the Church—as always, the absolute state's chief rival. Despite the warning of Our Lady at Fátima in 1917 concerning Russia, Bolshevik revolutionaries took control of that country later that year, killing the czar and his family. The Church was deprived of all lands and legal rights and an intense persecution of Catholics began, culminating in widespread Soviet genocide in Ukraine, Lithuania, Latvia, and Estonia. Across the ocean in the land of Our Lady of Guadalupe, an anti-Catholic socialist government enacted several persecutory articles in the 1917 Mexican Constitution, restricting the rights of the Church. Strict enforcement of these laws arrived with the presidential reign of Plutarco Calles in 1924: clergy were expelled, arrested, imprisoned, and executed, including the Jesuit martyr Bl. Miguel Pro (1891–1927). Governmental persecution led to a Catholic resistance known as the *Cristiada*, and though the ensuing civil war eventually ceased through diplomatic efforts of the United States, the Mexican government reneged on the negotiated settlement and renewed its persecution of the Church, spending decades hunting down the *Cristeros* freedom fighters.

In Spain, the Church was subjected to intense harassment in the 1930s when anti-Catholic political forces, bent on reducing the wealth and authority of the Church, took control of the government. A civil war erupted in July 1936 when the Nationalist leader Calvo Sotelo was assassinated, sparking a group of military officers into action. The nation divided into *Republicans*, consisting of a coalition of Marxists, socialists, anarchists, and virulent anti-Catholics, and *Nationalists*, who were conservatives, monarchists, and pro-Catholic. Republican attacks on Catholics were widespread and ferocious and resulted in the deaths of 6,832 priests and religious—twelve percent of the total Spanish clergy—including some who were martyred by wild animals in a public arena, a sight not seen in Europe since the Roman persecutions.[191]

In Italy and Germany, the rise of fascism and National Socialism posed significant crises for the Church. Pope Pius XI (r. 1922–1939) entered into a series of diplomatic agreements with these governments in an attempt to protect the Church and the faithful against persecution and safeguard its independence, but these gestures proved futile. The Fascists in Italy under Benito Mussolini, meanwhile, embraced a pragmatic relationship with the Church. Mussolini was a student of history and knew that secular rulers who attacked the Church had fared poorly. He noted, "[The] history of Western Civilization from the time of the Roman Empire to our days show that every time the state clashes with religion, it is always the state which ends defeated."[192]

Mussolini's more-sensible approach led to the resolution of one of the most pressing diplomatic questions of the day. The so-called "Roman Question" concerned the situation of the papacy vis-à-vis the nation-state of Italy. Since the end of the Papal States in the late nineteenth century, the popes had remained at the Vatican and withheld recognition of the new nation. The Lateran Treaty of 1929 resolved this diplomatic conundrum by creating the sovereign Vatican City state comprising 108 acres in the heart of Rome.

But despite a non-violent approach to dealing with the Church, Mussolini ran afoul of Pius XI in 1938 when Italy adopted the Nazi Nuremberg anti-Semitic racial laws. The pope expressed his extreme displeasure at the action when he told a group of Belgian pilgrims that "it is impossible for a Christian to take part in anti-Semitism. It is inadmissible. Through Christ and in Christ, we are the spiritual progeny of Abraham. Spiritually we are all Semites."[193]

The Church came under heavier pressure and attack in the Germany of the National Socialist German Worker's Party (Nazis). A concordat signed in 1933 was supposed to safeguard the rights of the Church and Catholics in Germany but the Nazis did not abide by its stipulations. The Nazis persecuted the Church by isolating and then abolishing Catholic labor unions, educational institutions, youth movements, and press. Attacks against the sanctity of marriage and family life, such as revised divorce and sterilization laws, were also conducted. Pius XI addressed the growing dire situation in Germany in his 1937 encyclical *Mit Brennender Sorge* (*With Burning Sorrow*), in which he attacked the core ideals of National Socialism, particularly its racist policies:

Whoever exalts race, or the people, or the state, or a particular form of state, or the depositories of power, or any other fundamental value of the human community, however necessary and honorable be their function in worldly things, whoever raises these notions above their standard value and divinizes them to an idolatrous level, distorts and perverts an order of the world planned and created by God; he is far from the true faith in God and from the concept of life which that faith upholds (8).

Although Pius did not mention Adolf Hitler by name in the encyclical, he criticized the Nazi leader and his cult of personality: "Should any man dare, in sacrilegious disregard of the essential differences between God and his creature, between the God-man and the children of man, to place a mortal, were he the greatest of all times, by the side of, or over, or against, Christ, he would deserve to be called prophet of nothingness" (17). The pontiff continued to demonstrate his displeasure with Nazi ideology, speaking out against the *Anschluss* (the Nazi annexation of Austria), Hitler's visit to Rome in May 1938, and the November 1938 pogrom known as *Kristallnacht*.

When Pius XI died the following year, the cardinals quickly elected the most capable candidate to succeed him. Eugenio Pacelli, who took the name Pius XII (r. 1939–1958), was well versed in events in Germany and in Nazi ideology. He had served as papal nuncio to Bavaria in 1917 and after the First World War was appointed nuncio for all of Germany. During his time in that nation, Pius XII witnessed the rise of Hitler and the Nazi party, and had criticized Nazi policies in forty public speeches between 1918 and 1929.[194] Pius XI had created Pacelli cardinal in 1929 and appointed him Vatican secretary of state. Throughout that tenure, Pacelli had continued to warn the world about the Nazis and their evil racial and political beliefs. Now as Pius

XII he issued a summons for peace, but his exhortation went unheeded as the Second World War exploded a month after his election. The German invasion of Poland in September 1939 resulted in the imprisonment and death of priests and lay Catholics along with the eventual massacre of millions of Jews.

During the war, Pius XII embraced the principles exhibited by Pope Benedict XV during the First World War: neutrality, constant exhortations for peace, and charity for all victims of the violence. His actions were applauded during and after the war, especially by Jewish organizations, and even though a later smear campaign of shoddy scholarship tried to paint him as indifferent to or even complicit in Nazi crimes, the authentic historical record credits Pius XII and the Church with the saving of hundreds of thousands of Jewish lives.[195]

The ultimate crisis inflicted upon the Church and world as a result of Modernism could be said to be the creation of *neo-paganism*. Like its ancient predecessor, this new paganism attacked the Church and its faithful—but this time it also focused its assault on the very foundations of Western Civilization. Rejecting divine revelation and divinely grounded objective truth and morality, the neo-pagan creates a world rooted in the individual with the belief that "man is sufficient to himself" and that his every whim and passion be afforded indulgence and "the practical permission of excess."[196] Neo-paganism rejects Christian teachings on marriage, sex, and family life, seeking to replace these things with perversions that produce a culture of death rooted in divorce, contraception, and abortion. Neo-paganism not only rejects Christian teaching but requires universal approval of depravity. What began as "isolated self-conscious insults to beauty and right living," Belloc writes, turned into "a positive coordination and organized affirmation of the repulsive and vile.[197]"

The crisis of neo-paganism crested over the Church just as many of the faithful themselves were rejecting Catholic doctrine and the practice of Christian virtue, at times even encouraged by the false teachings of the Church's own shepherds. Modernism seeped into the Church itself to such an extent that in some quarters previously accepted teachings were not only undermined but openly scorned. In universities and seminaries, teachers of theology and philosophy became agents of subversion, leaving their Catholic students indistinguishable from secular humanists. The militant Tridentine Church that had emerged from the Great Reform now found itself at a crossroads.

Renewal

Angelo Roncalli, the jovial seventy-seven-year-old patriarch of Venice, was a surprise choice as Roman pontiff upon the death of Pius XII in 1958. That wartime pope had expressed a desire, toward the end of this pontificate, to call an ecumenical council, but there was not much support for such a gathering among the papal curia and cardinals. Perhaps that offers one explanation for the choice of Roncalli, who took the name John XXIII (r. 1958–1963)—as his age seemed to preclude such a strenuous undertaking. However, much to the surprise of the curia, the cardinals, and the world, less than three months after his election John announced the calling of the Second Vatican Council.

Some within the Church believed there were no major problems requiring conciliar action, but the council planners saw a need to address matters that included the renewal of the liturgy with greater lay participation, reform of the Roman curia, relations with non-Catholic Christians, interactions between the Church and new nation states, the role of faith and science in the modern world, and the teachings of the Church vis-à-vis the modern industrial world, including moral problems associated with new technologies.[198] John XXIII recognized the desperate need for the Church to engage the modern world's brokenness with the peace and love of Christ and believed that ecclesial renewal was the key.

As part of the reform, John XXIII focused the tasks of the council on *aggiornamento* (literally a "bringing up to date"), *ressourcement* (return to the sources), and defense of the truth. The Church would be equipped to deal with modern culture and its challenges. It would return to the ancient sources of the Faith with renewed emphasis on Scripture and the writings of the Fathers. The hope was that the council would aid the Church not only in relationship with modernity but also invigorate it and the faithful.

In his opening address to the conciliar fathers, John XXIII remarked, "The Church, we confidently trust, will become greater in spiritual riches and gaining the strength of new energies therefrom, she will look to the future without fear" (*Gaudet Mater Ecclesia*). Since engagement with the modern world was a focus, the pope did not want the council to waste its energies on debating finer points of theology. Instead, the council was to focus on the presentation of the timeless teachings of the Church in the modern world. John XXII remarked that "the substance of the ancient doctrine is one thing, and the way in which it is presented is another."[199] The pope understood that modern man would not simply assent to the Church's teaching because it was proclaimed but rather wanted to know *why* he must believe the Gospel. So, John XXIII expected the council to explore new ways for the Church to express the validity its teachings to modern people immersed in the fruits of Modernism, especially religious indifferentism and skepticism. One new area of focus that would bear much fruit in the murky decades after the council was the vital role of the laity and their apostolate, particularly in the tasks of evangelization and catechesis.

The Second Vatican Council was the first ecumenical council in nearly a century and was the most attended ecclesial gathering in Church history. Its business was conducted over four sessions from October 1962 to December 1965; however, the man behind the vision of the council died in the summer of 1963 after the conclusion of the first session, and there was serious discussion over whether it should continue. His successor Pope Paul VI (r. 1963–1978) quickly silenced the question concerning the council's continuation by revising its statutes and outlining an agenda for its future sessions. All told, the council produced sixteen documents, among which were four major constitutions.[200]

Recognizing the evils of Modernism and the societal revolution produced by its fruits, the council urged the lay faithful to take an active role in the Church's mission. The laity have a unique opportunity to evangelize and make present the Church in "those places and circumstances where only through them can it become the salt of the earth" (*Lumen Gentium*, 33). In a secular and post-Christian world, the laity are given the special task to bring the light of Christ to those in the darkness, especially where modernity rejects organized religion and the power and authority of institutional churches. It is primarily through *authentically expressed Christian witness* that the laity can accomplished this special task. Modernism produces spiritual hunger, as people discover that neo-pagan principles do not satisfy their souls. In the dictatorship of relativism, modern man does not find answers to life's deepest questions. The world was ready for the truth of Christ witnessed afresh.

In its Decree on the Apostolate of the Laity (*Apostolicam actuositatem*), the Council urged the laity to be true apostles who look "for opportunities to announce Christ by words addressed either to non-believers with a view to leading them to faith, or to the faithful with a view to instructing, strengthening, and encouraging them to a more fervent life" (6). The Dogmatic Constitution on the Church,

Lumen Gentium, stressed that the fundamental call to holiness applies to *all* the faithful, regardless of vocation, and that the task of evangelization and catechesis is the purview of *all* the baptized, not just the clergy. In order to effectively participate in these endeavors and provide a witness to modern people, the faithful must know, live, and transmit the faith in accordance with their vocation. The council fathers urged the laity to utilize culture, media, and, particularly, their role in the procreation and education of children to renew the Church and civilization. They highlighted certain activities of the lay apostolate, such as the adoption of abandoned infants, marriage preparation, support for those in material and moral crises, and education, as vital tasks in the modern world (*Apostolicam actuositatem* 11). These tasks and the important role of the laity were further developed in the Pastoral Constitution on the Church in the Modern World (*Gaudium et Spes*).

This document was not only a response to Modernism but also was a clarion call to the Church and its faithful to actively engage modernity through the presentation of the Gospel and authentic Christian witness, noting that "the council yearns to explain to everyone how it conceives of the presence and activity of the Church in the world of today" (2). *Gaudium et Spes* first explicated the Church's teachings on the dignity of the human person, the call to communion with God, and the *law of gift* whereby man only finds himself through a sincere gift of self to another. These teachings are the antidote to offenses against human dignity prevalent in the modern world, such as genocide, abortion, euthanasia, torture, slavery, prostitution, human trafficking, and utilitarianism. Catholics were not to sit idle or become insular when faced with the problems of modernity but must take an active role in combating them by being engaged in the world and living the Faith in the public arena. The pernicious error, increasingly embraced by Catholic politicians of the day, of separating one's faith from public life was condemned.[201] Instead, the fathers encouraged all Catholics, and especially those occupying public office, to a unity of faith and life.

Gaudium et Spes also drew attention to two related areas of extreme important to the laity: marriage and family. The family, which is the foundational cell of society, faced grave danger in the modern world. Belief that God is the author of marriage and in the twofold purpose of marriage (good of the spouses and the procreation and education of children) was under considerable assault from modern forces. The growing availability and use of contraception and abortion posed a unique new danger for the health and stability of human society. As a result, Catholics were to work to preserve laws that safeguard marriage and the family and labor diligently to overturn those that sought to destroy it.

The Church's focus in this area continued after the council when Pope Paul VI promulgated an encyclical on the subject of married love and the transmission of life. Known as *Humanae Vitae*, the papal document reiterated the constant teaching of the Church concerning the truth and beauty of human sexuality in the midst of great societal and culture change. Issued during the midst of the Sexual Revolution, which sought to destroy Christian virtue and morality, *Humanae Vitae* emphasized the unique mission entrusted by God to married couples: to bring forth new human life as co-creators with him. At a time when the advent of the birth control pill, the ongoing shift from agrarian to industrial economies, and the relativism and dualism that accompanied Modernism were leading observers to predict that the Church would overturn its longstanding teaching on the integrity of sexual acts, Paul VI doubled down on it. Even as other Christian groups were abandoning their past prohibitions of contraception, with *Humanae Vitae* the Church affirmed that "each and every marital act must remain open to the transmission of life" (11).

Paul also responded to the needs of the modern day by reminding married couples of their duty to exercise "responsible parenthood," which could include learning about the biological processes of the body, especially the fertility cycle of women, toward making a "well-thought out and generous decision to raise a large family, or by the decision, made for grave motives[202] and with respect for the moral law, to avoid a new birth for the time being, or even for an indeterminate period" (10). *Humanae Vitae* was not just another moral instruction to Catholics; it was very much a fruit of the council in its invitation to the laity—to spouses—to witness Christian truth in their everyday lives. The invitation of *Humanae Vitae* was renewed and expanded later in the century through the catechesis of Pope St. John Paul II, who in his Wednesday general audiences developed the moral and sexual teachings of *Gaudium et Spes* and *Humanae Vitae* into his Theology of the Body.

Despite Pope St. John XXIII's hope that the council would produce a flowering of the Faith in the modern world, the decades after the council proved deleterious for the Church as religious observance and priestly vocations plummeted. Churches and schools closed. Many seminaries and Catholic colleges, some offering rationales wrung from the texts of Vatican II (or merely reference to its "spirit") gave themselves over to heterodoxy and perversion, and adherence to Catholic doctrinal and moral teachings plunged.[203]

But although the insidious ideology and heresy of Modernism produced a devastating crisis that radically altered human society and weakened the Church, it also prompted a vigorous response by the lay apostolate. Faithful laity throughout the world engaged in active ministry in efforts to share their faith, spread the Gospel, and combat the negative impacts of Modernism and neo-paganism. Sometimes with support from the hierarchy and clergy and at other times in spite of ecclesial malfeasance and neglect, new and vital lay apostolates in education, media, publishing, evangelization, catechesis, and apologetics flowered in the Church in the decades after the council and flourish still in our communication age.

This is not to say that there are no longer any problems in the Church or that the crisis of modernity in the Church has been eradicated. No doubt, there are still serious obstacles to the Church and its mission to the current day. The loss of faith in God and diminishment in religious practice, particularly in the Western world, with the concomitant increase in secular humanism, is most disconcerting. Modernist worldviews sadly even infects Catholics, including those in positions of authority within the Church.

So, where does this situation leave us today? The lessons of history get clearer the further back into the past you go. It is easier to discern the impact of reform movements and draw distinct conclusions centuries removed from the events. More difficult is seeing the long-term impact of recent events—events that *we are living and we ourselves are guiding*, today.

Only time will tell the full impact of the Catholic laity's engagement with modernity, upon which so much inside and outside the Church hinges. What the student of Church history can be certain of is the continued presence of the Holy Spirit, who guides, guards, and animates Christ's Mystical Body. Emboldened by his presence and trusting in the promises and grace of Christ, we faithful Catholics must continue to fight for the renewal and restoration of the Church—and likely, as Catholics of old did, to suffer for it. Let us all not waste the time and opportunities given us with fear or infighting; rather, let us take up the shield of faith and march boldly into the fray.

10

How to Respond to Crisis in the Church— and How Not To

I will reform my Spouse. I asked you to endure these sufferings, complaining of the iniquities of wicked ministers with you, and, showing you the excellence in which I have established these ministers, spoke of the reverence that I look for and desire from layfolk toward them. Answering you further, I explained how there was to be no lessening of reverence for them notwithstanding their failings, and how much any such thing was displeasing to my will.[204]

—Christ to St. Catherine of Siena

When faced with crises in the Church, Catholics have reacted in differing ways depending on the type of calamity, the societal and ecclesial norms of the time, their state in life, and their individual personality. Both reason and emotion informed their reactions and the steps they took to address the crises.

We Catholics today face our own ecclesial crises and we are influenced by the same complex factors as the faithful were in previous centuries—although with modern technology, both the amount of information and the speed with which it's dispensed are heightened, creating unique challenges. I think it can be profitable to examine how our elder brothers and sisters in faith dealt with Church crises, learning from them how to keep our faith—even grow in it—and maintain an even keel in the midst of trying times. Just as importantly, studying the actions of past Catholics can provide a cautionary tale against counterproductive and even spiritually harmful approaches.

In this final chapter we will look at the lives, times, and actions of two Catholics living in periods of great stress and crises within the Church: the Dominican friar Girolamo Savonarola (1452–1498) and the mystic and Dominican tertiary Catherine of Siena (1347–1380). May the example of these two fascinating individuals from our Catholic past lead us to a deeper love of Christ, his Church, and the sacraments; to the practice of charity in all situations; and to a rejection of pride, self-righteousness, and disobedience.

The Fiery Dominican

The Savonarola family hailed originally from Padua in northern Italy, where Michele Savonarola was a famous professor of medicine at the University of Padua. Michele attracted the interest of the marquis of Ferrara, who brought the doctor to the city as court physician. The family moved south, where Michele's son married a daughter from the rich and powerful Bonacossi family, which once ruled Mantua.

The union produced seven children (five boys and two girls). One son followed in the footsteps of the grandfather and became a doctor, another a professional soldier; and the other two, including Girolamo, became Dominicans. From an early age, Girolamo was exposed to the lifestyle of the rich and famous and the expression of political power, but he rejected the ostentatiousness on display in the Ferrara court and developed a severe austerity, rejecting material pleasures out of deep faith in Christ.[205] Graced with a brilliant and insightful intellect, Girolamo began studies at the University of Ferrara, but his mind turned to spiritual matters when he received visions of God calling him to proclaim the "ruinous state of the Church" and to work for its reform.[206]

Acting on a desire to reform the world and the Church, Girolamo fled Ferrara to Bologna, where he entered an observant Dominican house. His family was shocked at his actions, but he explained his decision in a letter to his father: "The reason that moves me to enter a religious order is this: first, the great misery of the world, the iniquity of men, the carnal crimes, adulteries, thefts, pride, idolatry, and cruel blasphemies."[207] Girolamo found his purpose and calling in religious life and took his final vows a year after entrance, spending his first years as a Dominican in Bologna, then being transferred to Ferrara for a few years.

In 1482, Savonarola was sent to the San Marco Dominican house in Florence as the chief instructor in theology and Scripture. He possessed an excellent intellect and an insightful mind with a gift for memorization, which served him well in preaching. The San Marco house was known as a group of Dominicans who lived as authentically as possible to the original regulations of their founder. Savonarola found kindred spirits in the monastery who pursued additional penances and disciplines and rallied against the material excesses in the world and Church. The reformist group was dismayed at the lax observance of other congregations and eventually sought and were granted separation from the Lombard monastery, which had served as the head of the northern observant Dominican groups. The San Marco community was placed in charge of a new Tuscan congregation, displeasing some Dominican houses that did not want to follow the stricter rules. Still, in Florence, the San Marco community grew in membership as men were attracted to its imitation of the original Order of Preachers.

In the late fifteenth century, the powerful and wealthy de' Medici family controlled Florence, a city of 40,000 people that was home to seventy international banking houses that produced a mass of profit for the city and its controlling families. These families constructed fortress-like domestic palaces to assert their identity and exhibit their affluence. These grand edifices of vanity drew the ire of Savonarola and his strict Dominicans.

As part of civic pride, Italian cities in the Renaissance competed against each other to attract popular preachers to give homilies during Advent and Lent. Preaching was an important civic activity; in fact, one of the main spectator activities of the time. Skilled orators, celebrities of their age who captivated large audiences with homilies lasting several hours, were in high demand. In 1490, Savonarola gave the Advent sermons at the San Marco house, in eighteen homilies attacking immoral clergy and Church corruption and criticizing the vain honors given to men merely on account of their wealth. These presentations led to an invitation the following year to preach the important Lenten sermons in the cathedral.

Savonarola took advantage of the opportunity and once more railed against the excesses of the day. He pulled no punches, claiming that Christ was speaking through him and viciously attacking lukewarm faith, ignorance of Church teachings, immoral priests, and the sins of simony and sodomy.[208] His topics were not confined to ecclesiastical abuses and sins against morality but encompassed political subjects such as unjust taxes and oppression of the poor. The Lenten sermons of 1491 brought Savonarola such fame and popularity among the lower elements of Florentine society that his critics complained he was the advocate of the "desperate and the malcontent."[209] The rich and powerful in the city, including the de' Medici, were not pleased with the preaching of the fierce Dominican, but they could do little to stem the growing enthusiasm and support for the man from San Marco.

Savonarola enjoyed preaching and believed he was called by God to use his gifts to reform the world and the Church. As his popularity increased, so did the boldness of his preaching. His homilies on the need for reform began with each individual Christian conforming his behavior to Christ and the teachings of the Church, which should then lead to collective reform in secular and ecclesial spheres. Savonarola believed that Florence should be a civic example to other towns: eradicating vices and vanities so that the city could be a beacon for a universal reform of the world and the Church. His preaching attracted a following of groups of young men who fanned through the city in search of objects of vanity. Known as the "San Marco boys" these groups brazenly knocked on the doors of Florentine homes hunting for playing cards, dice, chess sets, wigs, mirrors, dolls, cosmetics, perfume, costume masks and clothing, jewelry, and pornographic material.[210] Once acquired, the boys piled the objects onto large bonfires with celebrated zeal.

Savonarola preached not only against the excesses of the day but also on the coming divine judgment for the Church if it refused to heed his warnings and mend its ways. In provocative language he exhorted the Church to eradicate the prevalent abuses and corruption of the day:

Come infamous Church, listen to the words of your Lord: "I have given you splendid robes, but you have made them cover idols; I have given you precious vessels, but you have used them to exalt your false pride. Your simony has profaned my sacraments; lechery has made of you a pockmarked harlot. And you no longer even blush for your sins! Whore that you are! You sit on Solomon's throne, and beckon to all who pass you by. Those who have money you bid a welcome to and have your pleasure of them; but the man of goodwill is cast outside your doors!"

Savonarola's growing popularity led to his involvement in Florentine politics. The de' Medici clan's hold on power waned with the death of Lorenzo the Magnificent, the family's patriarch, in 1492—the same year that witnessed the election of the Spaniard Rodrigo Borgia as Pope Alexander VI (r. 1492–1503). A few years later at the encouragement of Ludovico Sforza, the duke of Milan, and several Neapolitan exiles, French king Charles VIII (r. 1483–1498) invaded Italy in order to take possession of the Kingdom of Naples by a distant claim from the Angevin side of the family. Charles raised a large army and marched into Italy.

On the way to Naples, the French approached Florence, provoking fear among the populace. Florence was perceived as an ally of Naples and people worried that the French army would conquer the city on its way south. Piero di Lorenzo de' Medici, son of Lorenzo the Magnificent, left Florence on a secret diplomatic mission to the French king. The chief ruling political body in Florence, the Signoria, had no knowledge of Piero's unauthorized outing. Several days after his arrival at the French camp, Piero sent word to the Signoria of Charles's demands, which were outrageous, and requested authority to conclude a treaty. Shocked at Piero's brazen unilateral diplomacy, the Signoria and two advisory councils refused the demands and eventually the de' Medici were exiled from the city after a tumultuous period of political uncertainty and threats of violence.

In an effort to undo Piero's disastrous negotiation, the Signoria sent a legation of six ambassadors, including Savonarola, to Charles VIII. The French king was enamored with the fiery Dominican, who viewed Charles as the instrument of God's vengeance and wrath on a sinful Italian people and the Church. Savonarola told the king that "your coming has lightened our hearts and exhilarated our minds" and that Charles was God's servant and agent of reform.[211] Savonarola believed firmly that material pursuits had so thoroughly corrupted Italian society and the Church that only a "divine scourging could cleanse and renew Rome, the Church, and Italy."[212]

With the de' Medici family exiled, other families and groups—including supporters of Savonarola and his observant followers—jockeyed for political power in Florence. The Dominican became involved in governmental affairs and attempted to implement reform policies and ideas in Florentine society. In his 1498 *Treatise on the Government of*

the City of Florence, Savonarola taught that secular government was stronger when recognizing the importance of
spiritual matters and engaging in religious activities. God
would certainly favor the city on the hill that provided an
example to others of righteous Christian living. Fifteenth-
century Florence had a reputation throughout Christendom
as a city of loose morals and especially rampant homosexuality.[213] That sin was so heinous in the eyes of Savonarola
that the Dominican preacher wanted violators to be stoned
and burned.[214] Although Savonarola enjoyed support from
many people, his fiery denunciations and uncompromising
demeanor unsurprisingly made enemies. Initially, opposition against Savonarola was localized in Florence, but as his
attacks widened to the universal Church, he drew the ire of
clergy in high positions of power and authority.

Reports began to filter to Rome about the firebrand
Dominican preacher in Florence. These reports included
claims that Savonarola believed Pope Alexander VI was not a
legitimate pope and that people need not obey him because
of the corruption, abuses, and immorality in his pontificate.
Savonarola certainly did criticize Alexander VI, and he even
preached about a future "angelic pope" sent by God who
would reform the Church and move the papacy to Jerusalem in anticipation of Christ's second coming: "The present Rome, that is, the wicked of Rome, will be reproved
and snuffed out, while the flower of Christians will be in
the region of Jerusalem . . . under one pope, Jerusalem will
flourish in good Christian living." [215] Savonarola argued that

his criticisms were born of loyalty and obedience; but despite his protestations, papal officials saw Savonarola as a threat.

The pope sent Savonarola a diplomatic letter in 1495 requesting his presence in Rome but the suspicious Dominican feared persecution and refused to go, feigning illness. The refusal to travel to Rome prompted a reply from Bartolomeo Floridi, a papal bureaucrat, sent to the Santa Croce congregation of Franciscans—no friends of Savonarola—in Florence. In a letter he severely criticized Savonarola, accusing him of having been "dragged to such a grade of madness as to proclaim himself sent by God and to be speaking with God."[216] The curial document ordered the reunification of the San Marco Dominican congregation (Savonarola's community) with the Lombard congregation, authorized Sebastiano Maggi, the Lombard vicar general, to initiate an investigation into Savonarola's writings and activities, and suspended Savonarola's ability to preach until the conclusion of the inquiry.

The Dominican was astonished upon reception of the letter. He replied to it the same day he received it, balking at the order for his community to be placed under the control of the lax Lombard congregation. Savonarola complied with the order to cease preaching, though, and for the next four months focused on writing. But when the Signoria took the bold step of ordering Savonarola to preach the 1496 Lenten sermons, he did so, in violation of the papal order. Meanwhile, recognizing the support Savonarola enjoyed in Florence, especially with the leading families and members of the government, Pope Alexander VI pursued a policy of patient tolerance of the friar's antagonistic preaching.

Savonarola continued to highlight the corruption and immorality at Rome, saying, "Once, anointed priests called their sons 'nephews'; but now they speak no more of nephews, but always and everywhere of their sons . . . O prostitute Church."[217] The pope sent Ludovico da Ferrara, the general procurator of the Order of Preachers, to Florence on a mission to convince Savonarola to stop his sharp rebukes of the pontiff. It is possible that a cardinal's red hat was even offered to Savonarola as a reward for softening his approach,[218] for in a homily soon after the visit, Savonarola proclaimed, "I want no hats, no miters large or small. I want nothing, unless it be what you [God] have given to your saints: death. A red hat of blood: this I desire."[219]

Although Pope Alexander VI was Christ's vicar on earth, Savonarola saw himself as Christ's vicar in Florence.[220]

Despite his lofty pretensions and plentiful support in Florence, many despised the Dominican and his teachings. His opponents included other religious, even Dominicans, who accused him of being an imposter, driven by ambition, power, and relishing in the celebrity status afforded him in Florence. His apocalyptic preaching themes prompted criticism and his speech sometimes drifted into areas of heresy and schism. Savonarola's supporters were called "wailers and bigots" by his enemies because they frequently cried during his sermons (Savonarola they called "Friar Big Onion"[221]) and zealously embraced his severe moral teachings. By

1497, the enemies were motivated to action. In May, some detractors broke into the Santa Maria de Fiore cathedral and smeared the pulpit with excrement, drove nails upward through the bookrest, and covered it with the carcass of a donkey.[222] Florentine authorities severely punished Savonarola detractors with exile, fines, and imprisonment.

After three years of patience, Pope Alexander VI finally had enough of the Dominican firebrand. On May 13, 1497, the pope excommunicated Savonarola on suspicion of heresy. Lifting this penalty required an appearance in Rome and an apology for his heavy-handed criticisms. Provided the means to soothe the situation and restore peace, though, Savonarola chose the path of resistance and disobedience. He published a letter in June addressed to "all Christians and the beloved of God" in which he declared that he was "sent by Jesus Christ to the city of Florence to announce the advent of the great scourging of Italy and above all of Rome, which is then to spread to almost all the world in our days and soon."[223] Savonarola wrote that although "the pope cannot err in the exercise of his office . . . if he commands a thing in error, he does not command as pope."[224] The critiques soon turned to all-out denunciations of Alexander VI as a false pope who "was not a Christian and had no faith of any kind."[225] He embraced the heresy of conciliarism, calling for an ecumenical council to depose the pope. Attacks followed against the papal bureaucrats whom Savonarola believed to be behind his censures.

After calling his excommunication a "diabolical thing made by the devil in hell,"[226] and firm in his belief of God's favor, Savonarola mounted a pulpit erected in front of the cathedral, raised the Blessed Sacrament, and exclaimed, "Lord, if my words are not yours, destroy me as I stand here now!"[227] The Lord did not destroy him, but Pope Alexander threatened Florence with interdict unless the excommunicated and defiant friar was muzzled.

Even while Rome's patience with Savonarola waned and the number of his opponents in Florence grew, the Dominican had maintained a high level of support among the citizens of the city—but that soon changed with an odd and comical event. The Franciscans in Florence were some of Savonarola's fiercest critics. Savonarola's claim that the papal bull of excommunication against him had no validity prompted the Franciscan friar Francesco da Puglia to challenge the recalcitrant Dominican to a public ordeal by walking through fire. (Medieval people believed firmly in the temporal judgment of God, and sometimes ordeals were undertaken in order to manifest a divine verdict on the guilt or innocence of the accused.) Savonarola rightly ignored the challenge, but without his consent a top assistant, Domenico Buonvicini da Pescia, accepted it. But the Franciscan da Puglia resolutely declared that he would undergo the ordeal only if Savonarola participated. As news of the challenge spread throughout Florence and the city buzzed in anticipation, another Franciscan, Giuliano Rondinelli, took da Puglia's place.

The two sides discussed the rules and procedures for the ordeal and finalized the articles of agreement in April 1498.

The article stipulated that if the Dominican participant refused to enter the fire, Savonarola would thereby agree to a sentence of exile. If both challengers were burned, Savonarola had three hours to leave the city. And if the Dominican survived, Savonarola's claims were vindicated.[228] The challenge was to take place on April 7 and workers prepared an elaborate structure in the government square: placing wood soaked with oil, pitch, resin, and gunpowder to ensure a huge conflagration. On the appointed day, Savonarola and his assistant da Pescia went to the square. The Franciscans raised a series of objections concerning da Pescia's clothing (he was wearing a cope), and his desire to carry a crucifix into the fire. Savonarola also brought the Blessed Sacrament to the event and suggested da Pescia carry the Host with him into the fire. The Franciscans strenuously objected to this idea and a heated debate between the groups erupted, lasting hours.

While the parties argued incessantly, rainclouds rolled into the area and a thunderstorm with hail and lightning scattered the people and soaked the wooden structure prepared for the ordeal. The people took it as a sign of God's disfavor toward the ordeal. They had expected a big show with a miraculous display vindicating Savonarola's preaching against corruption in the Church, especially the papacy, and when that did not materialize, they felt swindled and misled; the mood, once highly favorable, turned immediately sour toward the radical Dominican reformer. One day after the suspended ordeal—Palm Sunday—mobs marched to the

San Marco monastery issuing a summons for the Domini-can, shouting, "Kill the traitor!"[229] The Dominicans had stockpiled weapons as a contingency in case the Florentines turned on their cherished leader. A siege erupted and weap-ons were brandished, resulting in several deaths and many wounded on both sides. Realizing that his broad support among the populace and the government was over, and in an effort to avoid further bloodshed, Savonarola surrendered to Florentine authorities, who led him out of the monastery. The assembled crowd assaulted Savonarola, whose four years at the pinnacle of influence came crashing down in the span of a day.

The Signoria established a commission of seventeen lay-men, all enemies of Savonarola, to investigate the friar, which they did over a series of three trials. The secular authorities brought mostly political charges against Savon-arola and used torture during the first trial, which led to the Dominican's confession that his prophetic claims were not divine in origin. He confessed that "everything that I have done or planned to do was directed to my being famous in the present and future."[230] In the second trial, Savonarola admitted that he never went to the sacrament of confes-sion during the height of his power in Florence because he was not contrite for the sins committed in the service of his vision for reform in the world and the Church. However, now that he had been arrested, he recognized he was "a great sinner" and wanted "very much to confess rightly and to do heavy penance."[231] In the final trial, papal investigators asked Savonarola about a number of theological accusations, especially Savonarola's criticisms about the pope and denial of papal authority. The disgraced friar admitted to various wrongdoings and was declared guilty of schism and heresy and remanded to the secular authorities for punishment. The Florentine government convicted Savonarola and two of his associates and sentenced them to death. The three men were laicized, and on May 23, 1498, the former friars were hanged, their bodies burned, and their ashes thrown into the Arno River. Several days later, the government ordered copies of Savonarola's writings turned over to a papal envoy immediately under pain of excommunication.

There ended the sad story of Savonarola, whose scrupulosity and hatred of Renaissance vanities pushed him onto a stage from which he issued a summons of reform; but who, seduced by power and prestige, pursued a political agenda and placed himself outside legitimate ecclesial authority. Succumbing to pride, he abandoned faith in the Church's divine protection, believing that he alone possessed the answer to what ailed Christ's bride.

The Joyful and Determined Dominican

There was once a young woman who, like Savonarola, was devoted to the Order of Preachers, but the similarities between this spunky fourteenth-century mystic and that prideful fifteenth-century preacher end there.

Born on the feast of the Annunciation in 1347, Catherine was the twenty-third child of the wool dyer Jacopo

Benincasa and his wife Lapa. From a young age, Catherine was devoted to Christ and the Church. She wished to join a group of third-order Dominican women known informally as the *Mantellate* or "Cloaked Sisters" and formally as the Sisters of Penance of St. Dominic. The group of laywomen wore a white woolen dress with a white veil and black cape and lived in their own homes. Her family desired marriage for Catherine, however, and they persecuted Catherine in an effort to convince her to acquiesce to their plan. Her personal room was taken away and she was given a multitude of chores around the house to keep her so busy that she would have no time for prayer. Distraught at the behavior and unsure how to convince her family otherwise, on the advice of a Dominican friar Catherine cut off her hair to dissuade potential suitors.[232] Finally, she informed her family of the visions of Christ she experienced as a youth and her pledge of virginity out of love for him. This admission finally convinced her father that her desire to join the *Mantellate* was authentic and so the family acquiesced. Catherine joined the group in 1366 at the age of nineteen.

Catherine experienced a rich spiritual life from an early age, with locutions from Christ and visions of the Savior—the first when she was six—the Blessed Virgin Mary, St. Dominic, Sts. Mary Magdalen, John the Evangelist, Peter and Paul, and even King David. When she was still a little girl, a vision of the Blessed Mother prompted Catherine to request her assistance in remaining a virgin for life so that she could be espoused to Jesus. Her prayers were answered and when she was twenty-one, Jesus appeared to her and presented an invisible engagement ring as a sign of their spiritual union. Catherine could see the ring and it remained visible to her for the rest of her life, but it was invisible to others.[233]

Catherine's spiritual life included also great spiritual gifts and miraculous events. She had great concern for the sick and suffering in Siena, especially those afflicted with diseases that repelled others. Catherine cared for a woman afflicted with leprosy, which she contracted in her hands as a result. When the women died, Catherine buried her, and the leprosy miraculously left, and she was healed.[234] Catherine desired the salvation of all souls and interceded with the Lord on the behalf of others; for this, the Lord gifted Catherine with the ability to know the state of another's soul. This special spiritual illumination allowed Catherine to sense the "beauty or ugliness" of the souls in her presence but also those she could not see.[235] Souls in a state of mortal sin reeked in Catherine's presence. In the presence of Pope Gregory XI, Catherine would inform the pontiff that his court, "which should have been a paradise of heavenly virtues" was instead full of "the stench of all the vices of hell."[236] When in Avignon on a mission to convince the pope to return his residence to Rome, Catherine met a young beautiful woman, who was the niece of a cardinal. The woman could not look Catherine in the eye and when Bl. Raymond of Capua, Catherine's confessor, asked Catherine about the woman later, she told him the young woman, beautiful on the outside, reeked of decay. The woman was an adulteress and a priest's mistress.[237]

In 1376, Catherine received a spiritual gift from the Lord reserved to only a few holy saints: the *stigmata* or the wounds of Christ's crucifixion. But Catherine begged the Lord not to allow the wounds to be visible on her body, for fear they would attract others out of curiosity and detract from proper attention to Christ. He agreed, and so Catherine suffered silently with the wounds for the rest of her life; they became visible on her body only at death. In one of her many ecstasies, in which she was oblivious and impervious to the outside world, Catherine received a supernatural garment from Christ, which provided the ability to wear the same amount of clothing in winter or summer with no physical discomfort. Catherine wore a single tunic over a petticoat in all seasons thanks to this exceptional gift.

Catherine's spiritual life also included severe physical mortifications undertaken in order to subdue temptations so as to remain fully united with Christ. She practiced extreme fasting, whereby her confessor described her as "empty without but full within, dry to look at but inwardly watered by rivers of living water and at all times full of life and happiness."[238] She drank watered-down wine for a time, then switched to water for the rest of her life. Other physical mortifications involved sleeping on a wooden plank and a piece of wood for a pillow for only fifteen minutes a night; scourging herself with a rope three times a day; wearing a hairshirt and then an iron chain tightened around her waist;

and maintaining complete silence for three years speaking only to her confessor and to whomever he instructed her to speak with.[239]

These mortifications were not ends in themselves for Catherine but rather a means of focusing on heavenly rather than earthly things. Yet despite her spiritual focus and constant desire for union with Christ, Catherine engaged in affairs of the world. She dictated numerous letters to her dedicated assistants—since for most of her life she could not write. Although she was never taught to read and did not know Latin, Catherine was given the gift of reading the language and pronouncing the words properly.[240] She sent letters and answered inquiries from people throughout Christendom on various topics. She wrote to King Charles V (r. 1364–1380) of France exhorting him to rule justly, practice virtue, and love his neighbor, especially his subjects. Catherine's letters contained spiritual wisdom and encouragement and her scribes recorded her conversations with Christ uttered during ecstasies, which became her famous spiritual classic *Dialogue of Divine Providence.*

Affairs of the Church filled the contents of her letters as well. Catherine never ceased to issue calls for reform of the Church and for virtuous living on the part of the clergy, but those admonitions were always rooted in obedience, prayer, and trust in God's providence. She exhorted the faithful to constantly pray for the clergy, especially the Roman pontiff. In letters to the pope, Catherine encouraged him to select only virtuous men as bishops and cardinals so that they would provide worthy examples to the faithful and focus on spiritual matters. Failure to do so, she wrote, would be "a great insult to God and disaster to Holy Church."[241] Catherine had great love for the pope and referred to him in letters as "our sweet Christ on earth" and "daddy." Although always appropriately deferential, Catherine was also very direct in her correspondence with the pope. She urged him to refrain from focusing on politics, "for ever since Holy Church has aimed more at temporal than at spiritual things, matters have gone from bad to worse."[242]

Catherine lived during the time of the Avignon Papacy, when the papal residence and court was in southern France, causing great scandal throughout Christendom (see chapter 6). St. Bridget of Sweden (1302–1373) had worked tirelessly to end the scandal and bring the popes back to Rome, sending letters to the popes in Avignon urging their return. As we saw, she achieved temporary success when Bl. Urban V (r. 1362–1370) returned in 1370, but he remained only for a short time before the unstable political environment in Italy prompted his return to France. When St. Bridget died, the holy cause passed to Catherine, who wrote to the pope in one letter: "Come, come and resist no more the will of God that calls you: and the hungry sheep await your coming to hold and possess the place of your predecessor and champion, Apostle Peter. For you, as the vicar of Christ, should rest in your own place."[243] However, Catherine realized that letters were not sufficient to effect such a change, so she decided that a personal visit to France was necessary to bring Christ's vicar home.

Catherine and her confessor journeyed to Avignon and met with Pope Gregory XI (r. 1370–1378), a devout, modest, and virtuous man who was pleased to meet her. Since the pope did not know Italian and Catherine did not speak Latin, Bl. Raymond translated for the two. Catherine insisted that Gregory return the papal residence to its proper home and end the papacy's involvement in the ecclesiastical abuse of absenteeism, finally convincing him by reminding him of a private vow he had made to God as a cardinal: that if ever elected to the papacy he would move back to Rome.[244] But the task was not a simple one and there was much resistance. When news later reached Catherine that Pope Gregory was wavering in his decision to return to Rome, she wrote letters encouraging him to remain steadfast amid the storms:

I have prayed, and shall pray, sweet and good Jesus that he free you from all servile fear, and that holy fear alone remain. May ardor of charity be in you, in such wise as shall prevent you from hearing the voice of incarnate demons, and heeding the counsel of perverse counselors, settled in self-love, who, as I understand, want to alarm you, so as to prevent your return, saying, 'You will die.' Up, father, like a man! For I tell you that you have no need to fear. I beg of you, on behalf of Christ crucified, that you be not a timorous child but manly. Open your mouth and swallow down the bitter for the sweet.[245]

Gregory heeded Catherine's exhortations, rejected the counsel of his advisers who wanted him to remain in France, and left Avignon for Rome in the fall of 1376. The pope returned home in January 1377, thus ending one of the greatest scandals in Church history at the insistence of a simple pious laywoman from Siena.

Although successful in her mission to return the pope to Rome, Catherine was not pleased with the actions of Pope Gregory and the continued abuses in the Church. The setting may have changed from Avignon to Rome, but ecclesial behavior was no different. Catherine wanted Gregory to implement reform initiatives within the Church. When she did not see papal activity toward those goals, she wrote a scathing letter to Gregory: "Since [Christ] has given you authority and you have assumed it, you should use your virtue and power: and if you are not willing to use it, it would be better for you to resign what you have assumed; more honor to God and health to your soul would it be."[246] Note how, although her tone was direct and bold, Catherine maintained charity in her attitude toward the pope. Unlike Savonarola in the next century, Catherine did not question the validity of the papacy or pass judgment on the motives of the clergy but always clamored for change in charity and obedience.

Catherine recognized that a pope who implemented the necessary changes would meet resistance. She told Bl. Raymond that such a pope "will cause a scandal throughout the whole of God's Church, and the consequent schism will split the Church, and torment it like a plague of heresy."[247]

Sadly, Catherine's prophesy proved true in 1378 when Pope Gregory XI died and the Great Western Schism erupted.

Gregory's successor Urban VI (r. 1378–1389) believed that reform of the Church began at the top, and so he commanded the cardinals to change their eating habits and demanded absolute obedience to his reforms. Although these onerous methods might have been tolerated if issued by a saintly individual motivated by charity, they were intolerable coming from one who was "coarse, rude, and tactless to an extraordinary degree."[248] When news of Pope Urban's harsh measures and their effect on the cardinals reached Catherine, she wrote a letter urging the pope to "soften a little the sudden movements of your temper."[249] Unfortunately, Urban did not heed Catherine's warning, and five months after his election, fifteen of the cardinals who had gathered in April to elect Urban VI now met to declare Urban's election invalid and elected the antipope Clement VII. When she heard what the three Italian cardinals did in the invalid and illegal "conclave," Catherine sent them a stern letter:

You clearly know the truth, that Pope Urban VI is truly pope, chosen in orderly election, not influenced by fear . . . What made you do this? The poison of self-love, which has infected the world. That is what makes you pillars lighter than straw—flowers which shed no perfume, but stench that makes the whole world reek! Now you want to corrupt this truth, and make us see the opposite, saying that you chose Pope Urban from fear, which is not so.[250]

Catherine's fear of a great scandal in the Church caused by a reform-minded pope was realized, as the Great Western Schism lasted nearly a generation. She did not live to see the end of the schism she had prophesied, but she succeeded in her mission to return the pope to Rome and in calling the Church to reform because she focused firstly on her own spiritual life. Catherine was rooted in Christ and trusted and hoped in him. Everything she said and did was oriented toward Christ and how better to love and serve him. She was not interested in political power and prestige. She did not descend into schism and heresy like Savonarola because she pursued personal virtue and remained cognizant of her need for grace from the Church's sacraments, especially confession and the Eucharist. She was not fazed by the scandalous behavior of other Christians, especially the clergy, because she "was like a rock, established by the Holy Spirit in such great charity that no storm or persecution could unsettle her."[251]

Catherine and Savonarola had supporters and detractors during their lifetimes, but the impact these individuals had on them was markedly different. Savonarola reveled in the limelight brought by his preaching and was deflated when that support vanished after the failed ordeal. Catherine deflected all praise oriented toward her to Christ, even begging him to not give her spiritual gifts that would attract unwanted attention. She remained steadfast despite criticism and patiently and charitably endured all sufferings. Savonarola's popularity and fame were fleeting but Catherine's is eternal. The bonfires of the vanities stirred by Savonarola's inflammatory preaching were spectacles that prompted fascination and horror. Catherine gave the Church and the world an example of authentic piety, love of neighbor, and hope in divine providence. Contact with Savonarola produced extreme emotions of either support or opposition, but as Pope Urban VI remarked of Catherine, "None ever approached her without going away better."[252]

These two Dominican figures from past centuries provide compelling examples. We who are concerned about the actions of the clergy, corruption and abuse, and other problems in the Church should strive to emulate Catherine and reject Savonarola. An authentic Catholic response to problems in the Church begins with acknowledging the plank in our eye before highlighting the splinter in others. Focusing on individual reform and conformity to Christ will give us the tools to faithfully challenge and correct the abuses and problems in the Church. Prayer, virtuous living, trust and hope in divine providence, and respectful obedience to the hierarchy, as found in the life of St. Catherine of Siena, are the foundation of authentic Catholic response to crises in the Church. That foundation will effect genuine change and yield enduring reform in Christ's Mystical Body.

CONCLUSION

The lack of historical memory is a serious shortcoming in our society. A mentality that can only say, "Then was then, now is now," is ultimately immature. Knowing and judging past events is the only way to build a meaningful future. Memory is necessary for growth.[253]

—Pope Francis

In the Gospels, Jesus appears to make contradictory statements regarding the kingdom of God. The Lord indicates that the "kingdom of God is at hand" (Mark 1:15) but also says "my kingdom is not of this world" (John 18:36). Theologians struggled with reconciling these statements in relation to the Church and developed the understanding that the Church is the "already and the not yet." The Church is *already* the kingdom of God because some of its members, the saints, are in communion with God in heaven. But the Church is also *not yet* the kingdom because the visible element on earth is in constant need of renewal and will not fully be the kingdom until the coming of Christ again and the establishment of the new heaven and new earth.[254] This theological construct is helpful in reviewing Church history by providing a framework to acknowledge the Church's holy mission and actions but also the failing of its members and its constant need for renewal.

Since the Church on earth is composed of fallen yet redeemed creatures, the presence of crises should not surprise the student of history. Indeed, there has been hardly a time in the Church's history without crisis. From the question concerning the *lapsi* in the early Church to clerical sexual immorality in multiple centuries, to the troubled papacy with rampant corruption, secular interference, antipopes, to heresy, and to the influence of the modern post/ anti-Christian world, the Church has witnessed—and survived—quite a number of trials and calamities.

And what of today? Some liken the present situation to the time of Roman persecution, where a pagan, anti-Christian society openly and violently oppressed the nascent Church. Although the modern world contains elements of that early Church period as, sadly, Christians are still killed for their faith throughout the world, the situations are actually quite dissimilar. The modern Church exists in a pagan post-Christian world with its insidious problems of secularization, moral relativism, and cultural crisis. The Romans saw the Church as a new fad that sought to disrupt its society and bring forth political chaos,[255] and Christians were useful scapegoats for the emperors; but the Roman world did not persecute the Church primarily because it rejected its teachings and way of life.

There's another critical difference. Today, there are large numbers of Catholics who are *baptized non-believers* more influenced by secular humanism and anti-Christian sentiment than by the teachings of the Church. Robert Cardinal Sarah described these individuals as having "nothing Christian about them but the name. They still practice their religion but without conviction, as a purely cultural or social act."[256] There are many factors to explain this situation, but one cause is the disintegration of Christendom and the establishment of pluralism. Christopher Dawson noted the deleterious effects of pluralism on the Church and its members:

> [A] pluralist type of society involves serious disadvantages. It tends to make religion a matter of secondary importance. It means man's first duty is not religious but political. We do not ask whether a man is a good Christian or a good Catholic, but whether he is a good citizen or a good American. There is even a danger that it [religion] may be treated as a private hobby, so that a man's church membership will mean no more than his membership of a golf club.[257]

The embrace of pluralism and secularization leads to moral relativism where morality is viewed as a malleable human construct and not an objective truth given by the benevolent Creator—to which humanity must assent or face eternal consequences. The modern world has further rejected the Christian-built civilization rooted in the pursuit of authentic human freedom by following the commands of the Savior and the Church he founded. Instead, in its profound cultural and historical amnesia, modernity seeks to create a post-Christian utopia marked by license, tolerance, and pursuit of temporal pleasure. Yet perhaps more challenging are the *internal* issues the Church faces, such as the crisis of clerical homosexual abuse, which was developed and prolonged, in part, due to organizational structures within the Church that allowed sexual predators and abusers access to victims and freedom from secular prosecution.[258]

Some believe the modern crisis within the Church is the result of an infiltration of Freemasons, Modernists, liberals, or some other fifth-column group dedicated to destroying the Church from within. But the illness affecting the Church in the modern world runs deeper and is more perilous than the threat of nefarious groups lurking in the shadows. It is a "spiritual crisis, a crisis of faith . . . the mystery of iniquity, the mystery of betrayal, the mystery of Judas."[259] The betrayer of Jesus focused on worldly activities and the pursuit of prestige and adulation and criticized the expenditure of money on what he deemed valueless. Influenced by the Prince of Lies, he lied to himself, to his brothers, and to the Lord. He no longer believed but pretended to do so and sold the Savior for silver.

Despite disheartening crises, let us learn our lessons from Church history and not lose hope. Let us keep our eyes on Christ and on individual and communal actions that lead to eternal salvation. No, we should not ignore the need for temporal efforts or hide ourselves in bunkers. The laity, especially, should embrace past historical expressions of lay involvement in the Church. During the Catholic

Reformation it was not uncommon for devout laity to support the Church's missionary activity, to encourage bishops to remain steadfast in reform, and to hold the clergy accountable for their actions. A great example is Marie de Vignerot (1604–1675), the niece of Cardinal Richelieu (1585–1642), who financed evangelization efforts and supported the growing Church in Africa and Southeast Asia and worked closely with royal and ecclesial authorities in a respectful yet demanding manner.[260]

Yet we should also resist the temptation to focus excessively on temporal priorities, to remain hostage to the tyranny of the present, to "pretend to save the Church by our restructuring efforts, which only add all-too-human excess weight to her divine essence."[261] Keeping a properly balanced perspective will not only aid reform—it will guard us against undue anxiety and stress and the loss of faith that might result. Calamities affecting the Church from within or without, the actions of immoral and wicked clergy; they should not result in a loss of faith or hope or abandonment of the Church, but rather should prompt us to greater focus on prayer and hope. In prayer above all, in our "innermost respiration,"[262] we learn to persevere in the midst of great crises.[263]

Catholics of the past who persevered in crisis through prayer and hope did not always live to see the fruits of the reform they aided, but they always remained rooted in Christ and his Church. Let us imitate their example. Let us not sow fear, division, and discord, or become enamored of our own personal theories or solutions. Instead, let us trust in Christ, work toward our own and our neighbor's salvation, and remember that "we possess the hope that ensues from a real encounter" (*Spe Salvi* 32) with the God of faith, hope, and love.

St. Catherine of Siena and Mary, Star of Hope, pray for us.

ENDNOTES

1   It was common Roman practice to take children of prominent families from foreign tribes as hostages to ensure peace.

2   St. Augustine, *The City of God: An Abridged Version*, ed. Vernon J. Bourke (Image Books: New York, 1958), Book XIX, 465.

3   Henry Chadwick, *The Early Church: Revised Edition* (Penguin Books: New York, 1993 [1967]), 226–227.

4   Hilaire Belloc, *Survivals and New Arrivals: The Old and New Enemies of the Catholic Church* (Rockford, IL: TAN Books and Publishers, Inc., 1992 [1929]), 127.

5   Benedict XVI, Address at a Meeting with Young People, Cathedral of Sulmona, July 4, 2010.

6   Quoted in Desmond Seward, *The Monks of War: The Military Religious Orders* (New York: Penguins Books, 1995 [1972]), 222.

7   Cyprian, *De Lapsis*, 4. Maurice Bévenot, S.J., trans. St. Cyprian, *The Lapsed and The Unity of the Catholic Church*, Ancient Christian Writers, No. 25 (New York: The Newman Press), 16.

8   Robert Louis Wilken, *The Christians as the Romans Saw Them*, Second Edition (New Haven, CT: Yale University Press, 1984), 122.

9   Tacitus, *The Annals of Imperial Rome*, trans. Michael Grant (Penguin Books: London, 1981), 365.

10 See Robert Louis Wilken, *The First Thousand Years: A Global History of Christianity* (New Haven, CT: Yale University Press, 2012), 65.

11 See Philip Hughes, *A History of the Church: Volume 1—The World in which the Church was Founded*, second edition (London: Sheed and Ward, 1998), 97.

12 In the eastern part of the Church, there were identifiable stations for penitents undergoing *exomologesis* such as waiting outside the church and requested prayers of the faithful; remaining until the end of the homily; and staying for the entirety of the Mass. In the West, penitents were grouped with the catechumens.

13 See Wilken, *The First Thousand Years*, 68.

14 Cyprian, *De Lapsis*, 8.

15 Ibid., 10.

16 Hughes, *The History of the Church*, Vol. 1, 109.

17 Cyprian, *De Lapsis*, 27.

18 Ibid., 28.

19 Ibid., 34.

20 Ibid., 13.

21 The Donatists continued to be a thorn in the side of the Church. St. Augustine had to deal with them as bishop of Hippo during the fifth century!

22 Rodulfus Glaber, *Chronique*, Chapter XLVI (Paris, 1824). Quoted in Russell Chamberlin, *The Bad Popes* (United Kingdom: Sutton Publishing, 2004 [1969]), 67.

23 Gelasius, *Letter to Anastastius I.* Quoted in J. H. Robinson, *Readings in European History*, (Boston: Ginn, 1905), 72–73.

24 Sometimes referred to as the "Byzantine Empire." However, the German Protestant scholar Hieronymus Wolf (1516–1580) created that term in 1557. The "Byzantines" always saw themselves as Roman.

25 The art historian Sir Kenneth Clark referred to this practice as "hedging your bets." See Kenneth Clark, *Civilisation: A Personal View* (New York: Harper & Row, 1969), 14.

26 For more information on this myth and its fallacy see Thomas F.X. Noble, "Why Pope Joan?", *The Catholic Historical Review*, Vol. 99, April 13, 2013, No. 2, 219–238.

27 The reasons for the creation, development, and growth in popularity of the "Pope" Joan legend are discussed in chapter 6.

28 Quoted in Henri Daniel-Rops, *The Church in the Dark Ages*, trans. Audrey Butler (London: Phoenix Press, 2001 [1959]), 483.

29 See Russell Chamberlin, *The Bad Popes* (Sutton Publishing, 2003), 27.

30 Taking a papal name became the norm in the eleventh century.

31 Chamberlin, *Bad Popes*, 43.

32 See Liudprand of Cremona, *Works* (*Liber de Rebus Gestis Ottonis*), trans. F.A. Wright (London, 1930), Chapter X. Quoted in Chamberlin, *Bad Popes*, 57.

33 Named for the magician Simon Magus who attempted to purchase ordination from the apostles in order to receive the power of the Holy Spirit. See Acts 8:9–29.

34 Henry II was canonized in 1146, the only German monarch so recognized by the Church.

35 Chapter 3 highlights the pontificate of St. Leo IX, one of Henry's nominees.

36 The *Decree* is available in English translation in Colman J. Barry, O.S.B., ed. *Readings in Church History: Volume One—From Pentecost to the Protestant Revolt* (Westminster, MD: The Newman Press, 1960), 240–242.

37 Peter Damian, Letter 61 (Reindel, 2.208, trans.3.4). Quoted in

ENDNOTES

Kathleen G. Cushing, *Reform and Papacy in the Eleventh Century: Spirituality and Social Change* (Manchester, UK: Manchester University Press, 2005), 121.

38 Ordination of married men in the East continued through the centuries (and remains a practice) but from the seventh century onward only celibate monks or single clergymen were elevated to the episcopacy.

39 See Henry Chadwick, *The Church in Ancient Society: From Galilee to Gregory the Great* (Oxford: Oxford University Press, 2001), 358.

40 See Matthew Cullinan Hoffman, trans., *The Book of Gomorrah and St. Peter Damian's Struggle Against Ecclesiastical Corruption* (New Braunfels, TX: Ite Ad Thomam Books and Media, 2015), 10.

41 Hoffman, 82.

42 Ibid.

43 Ibid., 129.

44 See Hoffman, 18.

45 Hoffman, 149.

46 Ibid., 19.

47 See Warren H. Carroll, *The Building of Christendom, Volume 2—A History of Christendom* (Front Royal, VA: Christendom College Press, 1987), 472.

48 Peter Damian, *Vita beati Romualdi*, c. 35, ed. G. Tabacco (Fonti per la storia d'Italia, 94; Rome, 1957), 74–6; partial English trans. by H. Leyser in T. Head, ed., *Medieval Hagiography: An Anthology* (New York, 2000), 297–315. Quoted in Cushing, *Reform and Papacy*, 96.

49 Peter Damian, Letter 97 in Reindel, 3.67, 70–1; trans. 4.71, 74. Quoted in Cushing, *Reform and Papacy*, 117.

50 See Cushing, Chapter 2.

51 Ibid., 1.

52 See I.S. Robinson, trans. *The Papal Reform of the Eleventh Century: Lives of Pope Leo IX and Pope Gregory VII* (New York: Manchester University Press, 2004), 1–2.

53 Quoted in C. Morris, *The Papal Monarchy: The Western Church from 1050 to 1250* (Oxford, 1991), 125. Quoted in Eamon Duffy, *Saints and Sinners: A History of the Popes,* 3rd ed. (New Haven, CT: Yale University Press, 2006), 128.

54 Nearly 60 percent of the popes from 1073 to 1205 were monks.

55 See Cushing, 47.

56 Ibid., 48.

57 See Uta-Renate Blumenthal, *The Investiture Controversy—Church and Monarchy from the Ninth to the Twelfth Century* (Philadelphia: University

of Pennsylvania Press, 1995 [1988]), 73.

58 See the *Life of Pope Leo IX*, II.10 in *The Papal Reform of the Eleventh Century: Lives of Pope Leo IX and Pope Gregory VII* (New York: Manchester University Press, 2004),136–137.

59 *The Ecclesiastical History of Orderic Vitalis*, 5.12, ed. and trans. M. Chibnall, 6 vols. (Oxford, 1969–80), 3.120. Quoted in Cushing, *Reform and Papacy*, 15.

60 Brian Tierney, *The Crisis of Church and State 1050–1300* (Toronto: University of Toronto Press, 1988 [1964]), 51.

61 The term "oligarchy of warriors" is from Marc Bloch, *Feudal Society, Volume II—Social Classes and Political Organization*, trans. L.A. Manyon (Chicago: The University of Chicago Press, 1961), 443. The second quote is from Geoffrey Barraclough, *The Crucible of Europe: The Ninth and Tenth Centuries in European History* (Berkeley and Los Angeles: University of California Press, 1976), 86.

62 The word is modern with antecedents in a fifteenth-century treatise by the Italian Giacomo Alvarotto (1385–1453). The term *feudal system* was first used in eighteenth-century France. There is debate in the academic community about the term *feudalism* and its usage. See Susan Reynolds, *Fiefs and Vassals: The Medieval Evidence Reinterpreted* (Oxford: Clarendon Press, 1994) and Richard Abels, "The Historiography of a Construct: 'Feudalism' and the Medieval Historian", *History Compass* 7/3 (2009): 1008–1031.

63 Uta-Renate Blumenthal, *The Investiture Controversy—Church and Monarchy from the Ninth to the Twelfth Century* (Philadelphia: University of Pennsylvania Press, 1995 [1988]), 28.

64 See Bloch, *Feudal Society*, Volume II, 445.

65 Some historians argue that medieval people were not focused on this commonly portrayed "lord and vassal" relationship but rather on multiple types of relationships, such as "ruler and subject, patron and client, landlord and tenant, employer and employed, commander and soldier." See Reynolds, *Fiefs and Vassals*, 33.

66 See Marc Bloch, *Feudal Society, Volume I—The Growth of Ties and Dependence*, trans. L.A. Manyon (Chicago: The University of Chicago Press, [1939], 1961, 146.

67 See Blumenthal, 28.

68 J.H. Robinson, *Readings in European History*, (Boston: Ginn, 1905), 72–73.

69 Quoted in Bernard Guillemain, *The Early Middle Ages* (New York: Hawthorn Books, 1960), 44.

70 Translated in Ernest F. Henderson, *Select Historical Documents of*

the Middle Ages, (London: George Bell and Sons, 1910), 366–367. Available at https://sourcebooks.fordham.edu/source/g7-dictpap.asp. Accessed on December 23, 2020.

71   Clovis, King of the Franks (r. 482–511) was the first known to do so.

72   See Blumenthal, 28.

73   Ibid., 36.

74   Guibert of Nogent, *Memoirs*, 1.11, ed. J.F. Benton, *Self and Society in Medieval France: The Memoirs of Abbot Guibert of Nogent* (New York, 1970), 59. Quoted in Kathleen G. Cushing, *Reform and Papacy in the Eleventh Century: Spirituality and Social Change* (Manchester, UK: Manchester University Press, 2005), 14.

75   Quoted in I.S. Robinson, trans. *The Papal Reform of the Eleventh Century: Lives of Pope Leo IX and Pope Gregory VII* (New York: Manchester University Press, 2004), 87.

76   Letter of King Henry IV to Pope Gregory VII in *Readings in Church History: Volume One—From Pentecost to the Protestant Revolt*, ed., Colman J. Barry, O.S.B. (Westminster, MD: The Newman Press, 1960), 245.

77   Ibid.

78   Ibid.

79   *Register*, 3.10a. In Tierney, *The Crisis of Church and State*, 61.

80   Heribert, *Expositio in VII psalmos poenitentiales*, MPL 79, col. 626D. Quoted in Robinson, *The Papal Reform of the Eleventh Century*, 45.

81   A great personal friend of Pope St. Gregory VII and a supporter of the papacy in general, Matilda bequeathed her lands to the papacy in 1077 and again in 1112. When she died in 1115, her remains were buried in the abbey church near Mantua, but in the seventeenth century, her body was reinterred in St. Peter's Basilica in Rome in recognition of her defense of the papacy and life as a faithful daughter of the Church.

82   Gregory VII, The second deposition of Henry (March 1080), trans. E. Emerton, *Correspondence*, 149–152. Quoted in Tierney, *The Crisis of Church and State*, 65.

83   See Brett Edward Whalen, *The Medieval Papacy* (New York: Palgrave Macmillan, 2014), 99.

84   See Henri Daniel-Rops, *Cathedral and Crusade*, trans. John Warrington (London: J. M. Dent & Sons, Ltd., 1957), 180 for the Muslim troops in the Norman army and Tierney, *The Crisis of Church and State*, 55 for the extent of the fire.

85   Letter of Gregory to all the faithful (1084), ed. E. Caspar. *MGH Epistolae Selectae* II, 575. In Tierney, *The Crisis of Church and State*, 73.

86   See *Readings in Church History: Volume One—From Pentecost to the*

Protestant Revolt, ed., Colman J. Barry, O.S.B. (Westminster, MD: The Newman Press, 1960), 424.

87   *Sermo* II, PL 217 col 656. Quoted in Jane Sayers, *Innocent III: Leader of Europe 1198–1216* (New York: Longman, 1994), 91.

88   Letter to the prefect Acerbus and the nobles of Tuscany (1198) PL 214 col. 377. Quoted in Sayers, *Innocent III*, 197.

89   Jonathan Riley-Smith, *The Crusades—A History, Second Edition* (New Haven, CT: Yale University Press, 2005), 148–149.

90   See Daniel-Rops, *Cathedral and Crusade*, 139.

91   The phrase is Warren H. Carroll's.

92   Henri Daniel-Rops, *Cathedral and Crusade*, trans. John Warrington (London: J. M. Dent & Sons, Ltd., 1957), 520.

93   See Susan Reynolds, *Fiefs and Vassals: The Medieval Evidence Reinterpreted* (Oxford: Clarendon Press, 1994), 476.

94   See Jane Sayers, *Innocent III: Leader of Europe 1198–1216* (New York: Longman, 1994), 106.

95   See Edward Peters, *Torture,* expanded ed. (Philadelphia: University of Pennsylvania Press, 1985), 41.

96   Joseph R. Strayer, *The Albigensian Crusades* (Ann Arbor: The University of Michigan Press, 1992 [1971]), 3.

97   Ibid., 19.

98   Ibid., 23.

99   William of Puylaurens, *Chronicle*, trans. W.A. and M.D. Sibly (Woodbridge, 2003), 25. Quoted in Christopher Tyerman, *God's War—A New History of the Crusades* (Cambridge, MA: The Belknap Press of Harvard University Press: 2006), 575.

100 Warren Carroll, *The Glory of Christendom—A History of Christendom, Vol. 3* (Front Royal, VA: Christendom College Press, 1993), 165.

101 Strayer, 22.

102 Sayers, 156–157.

103 Quoted in Bernard Guillemain, *The Early Middle Ages* (New York: Hawthorn Books, 1960), 115.

104 See Walter Cardinal Brandmüller, *Light and Shadows: Church History amid Faith, Fact and Legend*, trans. Michael J. Miller (San Francisco: Ignatius Press, 2009 [2007]), 115.

105 Jews and Muslims were not subject to the inquisitor's authority since they were not baptized. In Spain, baptized former Muslims, who were suspected of practicing Islam secretly, were investigated by the Inquisition.

106 Bernard Gui, *The Waldensian Heretics* in James Bruce Ross and Mary Martin McLaughlin, eds., *The Portable Medieval Reader* (New York: Penguin Books, 1977 [1949]), 213.

107 Ibid., 214.

108 See Edward Peters, *Torture,* expanded ed. (Philadelphia: University of Pennsylvania Press, 1985), 57.

109 As an example, Bernard Gui passed 930 judgments in heresy cases during his career and only remanded forty-two obstinate heretics to the state for punishment. See Christopher Dawson, *The Formation of Christendom* (San Francisco: Ignatius Press, 2008 [1965]), 234 and William Thomas Walsh, *Characters of the Inquisition* (Rockford, IL: TAN Books and Publishers, 1987 [1940), 55.

110 See Dawson, *The Formation of Christendom*, 225.

111 Catherine of Siena, Letter to the Anziani and Consuls and Gonfalonieri of Bologna, *Saint Catherine of Siena as Seen in Her Letters*, ed. Vida D. Scudder (New York: E. P. Dutton & Co., 1906), 207.

112 See John Aberth, *The Black Death—The Great Mortality of 1348–1350: A Brief History with Documents* (New York: Bedford/St. Martin's, 2005), vii.

113 See Geoffrey Barraclough, *The Medieval Papacy* (New York: W.W. Norton & Company, Inc., 1968), 135.

114 Georges Digard, *Philippe le Bel et le Saint-Siège de 1285 à 1304* (Paris, 1936), II, 29; Franklin J. Pegues, *The Lawyers of the Last Capetians* (Princeton, 1962), 99. Quoted in Warren Carroll, *The Glory of Christendom—A History of Christendom, Vol. 3* (Front Royal, VA: Christendom College Press, 1993), 334.

115 See Brian Tierney, *The Crisis of Church and State 1050–1300* (Toronto: University of Toronto Press, 1988 [1964]), 173.

116 Boniface VIII, *Ausculta fili* in Tierney, *The Crisis of Church and State*, 186.

117 Quoted in Henri Daniel-Rops, *Cathedral and Crusade*, trans. John Warrington (London: J. M. Dent & Sons, Ltd., 1957), 573.

118 See Yves Renouard, trans. Denis Bethell, *The Avignon Papacy: The Popes in Exile 1305–1403* (New York: Barnes & Noble Books, 1994 [1954]), 35. The city's population grew to 30,000 from 5,000 by the end of the papal stay in 1376. See Renouard, 93.

119 See Brett Edward Whalen, *The Medieval Papacy* (New York: Palgrave Macmillan, 2014), 161.

120 Renouard, 37.

121 See Sigrid Undset, *Catherine of Siena*, trans., Kate Austin-Lund (San Francisco: Ignatius Press, 2009 [1954]), 210.

122 See Renouard, 64.

123 Additional details on how Catherine interacted with the pope are provided in Chapter 9.

124 See Henri Daniel-Rops, *The Protestant Reformation*, Vol. 1, trans. Audrey Butler (New York: Image, 1963), 45.

125 Quoted in Barraclough, *The Medieval Papacy*, 158.
126 Ibid., 171.
127 Martin V did not implement these conciliar decrees and the heresy of conciliarism was condemned by Pope Pius II in 1460 and again at the Fifth Lateran Council in the sixteenth century.
128 See Barraclough, *The Medieval Papacy*, 126.
129 See Jamie Blosser, *Positively Medieval—The Surprising, Dynamic, Heroic Church of the Middle Ages* (Huntington, IN: Our Sunday Visitor, 2016), 190.
130 Quoted in Blosser, *Positively Medieval*, 195.
131 Henri Daniel-Rops, *The Protestant Reformation*, Vol. 1, trans. Audrey Butler (New York: Image, 1963), 336.
132 The word means "rebirth" in French and was first used by Jean Michelet (1798–874) in his book *History of France* in 1855. The term describes the cultural activity in Europe (principally in Italy) beginning in the fifteenth century that imitated ancient Greek and Roman art, architecture, literature, and philosophy.
133 Geoffrey Barraclough, *The Medieval Papacy* (New York: W.W. Norton & Company, Inc., 1968), 91.
134 Commonly known as the Sistine Chapel for Sixtus IV.
135 E.R. Chamberlin, *The Fall of the House of Borgia* (New York, 1974), 49. Quoted in Warren Carroll, *The Glory of Christendom—A History of Christendom, Vol. 3* (Front Royal, VA: Christendom College Press, 1993), 639.
136 Michael Mallett, *The Borgias: The Rise and Fall of a Renaissance Dynasty* (New York, 1969), 118–120. Quoted in Carroll, *The Glory of Christendom*, 639.
137 See Chapter 9.
138 Quoted in Daniel-Rops, *The Protestant Reformation*, Vol. 1., 309.
139 Quoted in Brett Edward Whalen, *The Medieval Papacy* (New York: Palgrave Macmillan, 2014), 192.
140 See Robert Royal, *The Pope's Army: 500 Years of the Papal Swiss Guard* (New York: Crossroads, 2006), 36.
141 Daniel-Rops, *The Protestant Reformation*, Vol. 1, 340.
142 Quoted in Barraclough, *The Medieval Papacy*, 161.
143 See Yves Renouard, trans. Denis Bethell, *The Avignon Papacy: The Popes in Exile 1305–1403* (New York: Barnes & Noble Books, 1994 [1954]), 133.
144 Although the abuses posed problems for the Church and negatively impacted people's view of it, the Protestant narrative that the Church was so corrupt that it could only be reformed by the actions of brave men

such as Martin Luther and John Calvin is false. For more information on refuting the standard Protestant narrative see my book *The Real Story of Catholic History: Answering Twenty Centuries of Anti-Catholic Myths* (El Cajon: Catholic Answers Press, 2017), chapter 26.

145　Eamon Duffy, *Saints and Sinners: A History of the Popes* (New Haven, CT: Yale University Press, 2006), 198.

146　Hilaire Belloc, *The Great Heresies* (Rockford, IL: TAN Books and Publishers, Inc., 1991 [1938]), 110.

147　Ulrich von Hutton, *The Roman Trinity.* Quoted in Roland H. Bainton, *Here I Stand: A Life of Martin Luther* (New York: Mentor Books, 1950), 101.

148　G.K. Chesterton, *The Resurrection of Rome, CW* 21:349–350. Quoted in G.K. Chesterton, *Lepanto,* ed. Dale Ahlquist (San Francisco: Ignatius Press, 2004, 85.

149　The treatises were *Appeal to the Christian Nobility of the German Nation* (August 1520), *The Babylonian Captivity of the Church* (October 1520), and *A Treatise on Christian Liberty* (November 1520).

150　Quoted in Bainton, *Here I Stand: A Life of Martin Luther,* 145.

151　The phrase is Hilaire Belloc's. See Hilaire Belloc, *How the Reformation Happened* (Rockford, IL: TAN Books and Publishers, 1992 [1928]), 79.

152　Philip Hughes, *A Popular History of the Reformation* (New York: Image Books, 1960), 153.

153　In classical Protestant teaching, the rule of faith was up to each individual's private interpretation of Scripture; in practice, of course, different Protestant leaders and groups developed their own orthodoxies of doctrine and worship and required adherence.

154　See Hilaire Belloc, *How the Reformation Happened,* 175–178.

155　See Brad S. Gregory, *The Unintended Reformation: A Religious Revolution Secularized Society* (Cambridge, MA: Harvard University Press, 2012).

156　The Catholic Reformation (1545–1700) is usually referred to as the "Counter-Reformation," but this is a Protestant term meant to convey the notion that the Church "undid" the great reform ushered in by Luther, Calvin, and other revolutionaries. Authentic reform seeks to renew and restore, not destroy and replace; thus, it is best to use the term "Catholic Reformation" because it was the movement of authentic reform undertaken by the Church.

157　Hubert Jedin, *A History of the Council of Trent,* Vol. I (St. Louis, 1957), 577. Quoted in Warren H. Carroll, *The Cleaving of Christendom: A History of Christendom, Volume 4* (Front Royal, VA: Christendom Press, 2000), 191.

158 Henri Daniel-Rops, trans. John Warrington, *The Catholic Reformation: Volume 1* (Garden City, NY: Image Books, 1964), 189.

159 Ibid., 153.

160 Ignatius and his companions vowed initially to go to Jerusalem on an evangelization mission to convert Muslims but were unsuccessful in journeying to the Holy Land. They traveled to Rome instead where they placed themselves under direct obedience to the pope.

161 The other six martyrs were René Goupil (1608–1642), Jean de la Lande (d. 1646), Antoine Daniel (1601–1648), Gabriel Lalement (1610–1649), Charles Garnier (1606–1649), and Nöel Chabanel (1613–1649).

162 The first apostle of Germany was the martyr St. Boniface (680–754).

163 The canonizations were the first in sixty-five years and involved Teresa of Ávila, Philip Neri, Ignatius Loyola, and Francis Xavier. St. Isidore the Farmer (1070–1130) was also canonized that day.

164 Henri Daniel-Rops, *The Catholic Reformation*, Vol. 2, trans. John Warrington (New York: Image Books, 1964 [1955]), 218.

165 John Paul II, *Memory and Identity: Conversations at the Dawn of a Millennium* (New York: Rizzoli, 2005), 10.

166 Thomas Paine, the American War of Independence propagandist and author of *Common Sense*, coined the term "Age of Reason" while in prison in Paris in 1793–1794. See Rodney Stark, *Bearing False Witness: Debunking Centuries of Anti-Catholic History* (West Conshohocken, PA: 2016), 91.

167 In that month October 4 was followed by October 15. The revised calendar became known as the Gregorian calendar and is still used today.

168 See Joshua 10:12–14 and Psalm 92:1.

169 Jerome L. Langford, *Galileo, Science, and the Church,* 3rd ed. (Ann Arbor: University of Michigan Press, 1992), 90. The ruling, with the eyes of hindsight, was imprudent and a scientific matter not within the competency of the Inquisition.

170 The quote is from Voltaire. See Maurice A. Finocchiaro, "Myth 8: That Galileo Was Imprisoned and Tortured for Advocating Copernicanism." In *Galileo Goes to Jail: And Other Myths About Science and Religion*, edited by Ronald L. Numbers (Cambridge, MA: Harvard University Press, 2009), 68. Quoted in Stark, *Bearing False Witness*, 135.

171 Stanley L. Jaki, *Galileo Lessons* (Pinckney, MI: Real View Books, 2001), 17.

172 See Stark, *Bearing False Witness*, 144. Some examples of these Catholic scientists include: Robert Grosseteste (1168–1253), an English bishop,

who made contributions to optics, physics and astronomy; St. Albert the Great (1206–1280), a Dominican university professor and teacher of St. Thomas Aquinas, who was an expert in botany and made advances in geography, astronomy and chemistry; Roger Bacon (1214–1294), a Franciscan, who contributed to the knowledge of mathematics, astronomy, the physiology of eyesight, optics, eye-glasses, and concocted a recipe for gunpowder; and, Nicole D'Oresme (1325–1382), the bishop of Lisieux, who established that the earth turns on its axis. Additionally, many fields of science owe their origin to the work of Catholic clergy. The fathers of geology (Nicolaus Steno, 1638–1686), Egyptology (Athanasius Kircher, 1602–1680), and modern atomic theory (Roger Boscovich, 1711–1787) were Catholic priests and the father of genetics, Gregor Mendel (1822–1884) was an Augustinian friar.

173 For Descartes, if doubt reigned supreme, then the only certain thing was doubt and so the only clear and distinct idea that cannot be doubted is the fact that one is thinking, which proves one's existence: Cogito, ergo sum.

174 Martin P. Harney, *The Jesuits in History* (New York, 1941), 292. Quoted in Warren H. Carroll and Anne Carroll, *The Revolution against Christendom: A History of Christendom, Volume 5* (Front Royal, VA: Christendom Press, 2005), 83.

175 Clement XIV, *Dominus ac Redemptor.* Quoted in G.B Nicolini, *History of the Jesuits: Their Origin, Progress, Doctrines and Designs* (George Bell & Co., London & New York, 1893).

176 Pope Pius VII (r. 1800–1823) re-established the Society on August 7, 1814.

177 See Walter Cardinal Brandmüller, *Light & Shadows: Church History amid Faith, Fact and Legend*, trans. Michael J. Miller (San Francisco, CA: Ignatius Press, 2009), 190.

178 Warren H. Carroll and Anne W. Carroll, *The Crisis of Christendom: Volume VI in A History of Christendom* (Front Royal, VA: Christendom Press, 2013), 1.

179 Brennan Pursell, *History in His Hands: A Christian Narrative of the West* (New York: Crossroad, 2011), 200.

180 French society was divided into three estates as follows: First Estate (clergy), Second Estate (nobility), and Third Estate (commoners).

181 Contrary to popular belief, the Bastille was not important to the monarchy as it was considered for demolition due to high maintenance costs.

182 The guards initially fought bravely but were ordered to lay down their arms by the king. See Warren H. Carroll and Anne Carroll,

The Revolution against Christendom: A History of Christendom, Volume 5 (Front Royal, VA: Christendom Press, 2005), 154. The famous Lion Monument in Lucerne, Switzerland, (a nineteenth-century rock relief carving into the cliff face of a former quarry featuring a dying lion), commemorates the fallen Swiss Guards.

183 See Reynald Secher, *A French Genocide—The Vendée*, trans. George Holoch (Notre Dame, IN: University of Notre Dame Press, 2003 [1986]), 212.

184 Christopher Hibbert, *Garibaldi and His Enemies* (Boston, 1966), 36–37. Quoted in Carroll, *The Crisis of Christendom*, 119–120.

185 See Carroll and Carroll, *The Crisis of Christendom*, 121.

186 Philip Hughes, *The Church in Crisis: A History of the General Councils 325–1870* (New York: Doubleday, 1961), 340.

187 George J. Marlin, "The Original Culture War," *The Catholic Thing*, May 18, 2011. Available online at https://www.thecatholicthing. org/2011/05/18/the-original-culture-war/. Accessed May 30, 2021.

188 Hilaire Belloc, *The Great Heresi*es (Rockford, IL: TAN Books and Publishers, Inc., 1991 [1938], 159.

189 See Warren H. Carroll and Anne W. Carroll, *The Crisis of Christendom: A History of Christendom, Volume 6* (Front Royal, VA: Christendom Press, 2013), 257.

190 Steven Ozment, *A Mighty Fortress: A New History of the German People* (New York: HarperCollins Publishers, 2004), 240.

191 Numbers of deaths and destruction of churches from Warren H. Carroll, *The Last Crusade: Spain: 1936* (Front Royal, VA: Christendom Press, 1996), 212 & 213. Account of priests killed by wild animals in Robert Royal, *The Catholic Martyrs of the Twentieth Century: A Comprehensive World History* (New York: The Crossroad Publishing Company, 2000), 125.

192 Camille Cianfarra, *The Vatican and the War* (New York: E.P. Dutton & Company, 1944), 69. Quoted in Ronald J. Rychlak, *Hitler, the War, and the Pope* (Huntington, IN: Our Sunday Visitor, 2000), 35.

193 https://www.ccjr.us/dialogika-resources/primary-texts-from-the-history-of-the-relationship/pius-xi1938sept6#ges:searchword%3Dpius%2Bxi%26searchphrase%3Dall%26page%3D1. Accessed January 26, 2021.

194 David G. Dalin, *The Myth of Hitler's Pope: How Pope Pius XII Rescued Jews from the Nazis* (Washington, D.C.: Regnery Publishing, Inc., 2005), 63.

195 The Jewish historian Pinchas E. Lapide estimated that Pius XII and the Church rescued 860,000 Jewish lives from the Nazis, representing 37 percent of Jews who survived the war. See Lapide, *Three Popes and*

the Jews (New York: Hawthorn Books, Inc., 1967), 215.

196 Hilaire Belloc, *Survivals and New Arrivals: The Old and New Enemies of the Catholic Church* (Rockford, IL: TAN Books and Publishers, Inc., 1992 [1929]), 141.

197 Ibid., 136.

198 See Joseph Ratzinger, *Theological Highlights of Vatican II* (New York: Paulist Press, 1966), Kindle edition, location 937.

199 Ibid.

200 The four major constitutions are Sacrosanctum Concilium (1963), Lumen Gentium (1964), Dei Verbum (1965), and Gaudium et Spes (1965).

201 "This split between the faith which many profess and their daily lives deserves to be counted among the more serious errors of our age" (43).

202 "*seriis causis.*"

203 Eleven years after the council, it was estimated that as many as 10 million Catholics in the United States alone ceased regular attendance at Sunday Mass, a 30 percent decrease from before the council. A survey conducted in 1976 indicated seven out of ten Catholics approved of legalized abortion; eight out of ten approved of artificial means of birth control; and four out of ten did not believe in papal infallibility. See Msgr. George Kelly, *The Battle for the American Church* (New York: Doubleday & Company, Inc., 1979), 456–457. Sadly, more recent studies show significant heterodox belief and practice by Catholics in the United States. See https://www.pewresearch.org/fact-tank/2019/08/05/transubstantiation-eucharist-u-s-catholics/.

204 Bl. Raymond of Capua, *The Life of St. Catherine of Siena*, trans. George Lamb (Charlotte, NC: TAN Books, 2011 [1934], 295.

205 See his poems De ruina mundi (On the Ruin of the World) and De ruina ecclesiae (On the Ruin of the Church).

206 Henri Daniel-Rops, *The Protestant Reformation*, Vol. 1, trans. Audrey Butler (New York: Image, 1963), 311.

207 Quoted in Lauro Martines, *Fire in the City: Savonarola and the Struggle for Renaissance Florence* (New York: Oxford University Press, 2006), 12.

208 Martines, 27.

209 Ibid., 32.

210 Ibid., 116.

211 Ibid., 50.

212 Ibid., 93.

213 Indeed, the German term for sodomy at the time was Florenzen.

214 Martines, 693.

215 *Select Writings of Girolamo Savonarola: Religion and Politics, 1490–1498*, ed. and trans. A. Borelli and M.P. Passaro (New Haven, CT: Yale University Press, 2006), 287. Quoted in Brett Edward Whalen, *The Medieval Papacy* (New York: Palgrave Macmillian, 2014), 191.

216 Quoted in Martines, 128.

217 J.C. Olin (ed.), *The Catholic Reformation: Savonarola to Ignatius Loyola* (Westminster, MD, 1969), 9. Quoted in Eamon Duffy, *Saints and Sinners: A History of the Popes,* 3rd ed. (New Haven, CT: Yale University Press, 2006), 197.

218 Some historians dispute the claim Savonarola was offered a red hat. See Martines, 137.

219 Quoted in Martines, 137.

220 Martines, 140.

221 Ibid., 158.

222 Ibid., 1.

223 Ibid., 173.

224 Ibid., 174.

225 See Daniel-Rops, *The Protestant Reformation*, Vol. 1, 317 and Martines, 207.

226 Martines, 206.

227 Daniel-Rops, *The Protestant Reformation*, Vol. 1, 317.

228 Martines, 222.

229 Ibid., 233.

230 Ibid., 254.

231 Ibid., 255

232 Bl. Raymond of Capua, *The Life of St. Catherine of Siena*, trans. George Lamb (Charlotte, NC: TAN Books, 2011 [1934], 25.

233 Ibid., 82.

234 Ibid., 114.

235 Ibid., 118.

236 Ibid., 119–120.

237 See Sigrid Undset, *Catherine of Siena*, trans., Kate Austin-Lund (San Francisco: Ignatius Press, 2009 [1954]), 77.

238 Bl. Raymond of Capua, *The Life of St. Catherine of Siena*, 136.

239 See Bl. Raymond of Capua, *The Life of St. Catherine*, 11, 23, 37, 54.

240 Bl. Raymond of Capua, *The Life of St. Catherine of Siena*, 79.

241 Catherine of Siena, *Letter to Gregory XI, Saint Catherine of Siena as Seen in Her Letters*, ed. Vida D. Scudder (New York: E. P. Dutton & Co., 1906), 122.

242 Ibid., 129.

243 Ibid., 128.

ENDNOTES

244 See Sigrid Undset, *Catherine of Siena*, trans., Kate Austin-Lund (San Francisco: Ignatius Press, 2009 [1954]), 210.

245 Catherine of Siena, *Letter to Gregory XI*, *Saint Catherine of Siena as Seen in Her Letters*, ed. Vida D. Scudder (New York: E. P. Dutton & Co., 1906), 165–166, and 185.

246 Ibid., 234.

247 Bl. Raymond of Capua, *The Life of St. Catherine of Siena*, 232.

248 Renouard, *The Avignon Papacy*, 69.

249 Philip Hughes, *A Popular History of the Catholic Church* (New York: Image, 1947), 144.

250 Catherine of Siena, *Letter to Three Italian Cardinals* in Scudder, 278.

251 Bl. Raymond of Capua, *The Life of St. Catherine of Siena*, 341.

252 Ibid., xiii.

253 *Amoris Laetitia*, 193.

254 See *Lumen Gentium*, 5.

255 See Robert Louis Wilken, *The Christians as the Romans Saw Them*, Second Edition (New Haven, CT: Yale University Press, 1984).

256 Robert Cardinal Sarah, *The Day is Now Far Spent*, with Nicholas Diat, trans. Michael J. Miller (San Francisco: Ignatius Press, 2019), 293.

257 Christopher Dawson, *The Formation of Christendom* (San Francisco: Ignatius Press, 2008 [1965]), 20.

258 An excellent article that explores how modern Church organizational structures produced a leadership crisis that fueled the sex abuse crisis is Bronwen McShea, "Bishops Unbound: The History Behind Today's Crisis of Church Leadership," *First Things*, January 2019.

259 Robert Cardinal Sarah, *The Day is Now Far Spent*, 12.

260 See Bronwen McShea, "Bishops Unbound: The History Behind Today's Crisis of Church Leadership," *First Things*, January 2019.

261 Ibid., 114.

262 Robert Cardinal Sarah, *The Day is Now Far Spent*, 16.

263 Benedict XVI, *Spe Salvi*, 32.

ABOUT THE AUTHOR

Steve Weidenkopf teaches at the Christendom College Graduate School of Theology. He is the author of *The Church and the Middle Ages: 1000-1378* (2020); *Timeless: A History of the Catholic Church* (2019); *The Real Story of Catholic History: Answering Twenty Centuries of Anti-Catholic Myths* (2017); *The Glory of the Crusades* (2014); and is the creator and co-author of *Epic: A Journey Through Church History* and the author of *The Early Church* adult faith formation studies. Steve is a member of the Society for the Study of the Crusades and the Latin East, an international academic group dedicated to the field of Crusading history. He is also a Knight of the Equestrian Order of the Holy Sepulchre of Jerusalem. Steve and his wife live in Northern Virginia and are blessed with six children and one grandchild.